YEARS OF BLOOD

﴾ قانلو سنه لر ﴿

۱۳۲۳ نجی سنهٔ هجریه ده (۱۹۰۵ سنهٔ میلادیه ده) قافقازده سرزده
ظهور اولان ارمنی مسلمان دعواسنك تاریخی

اثر: محمد سعید اوردوبادی

باکو ثروتدارلریندن آقا مرتضی مختاروفك اعانه سیله طبع اولوندی

هاشم بك وزیر اوفك «صدا» مطبعه سنده ۱۹۱۱

YEARS OF BLOOD

A History of the Armenian-Muslim Clashes
in the Caucasus, 1905-1906

MAMMAD SAID ORDUBADI

EDITOR
Tale Heydarov

EDITORIAL BOARD
Taleh Baghiyev, Kerim Shukurov (Footnotes and Index)
Ian Peart, Qilinjkhan Bayramov (Translation)

YEARS OF BLOOD
A History of the Armenian-Muslim Clashes in the Caucasus, 1905-1906

Published by
Ithaca Press
8 Southern Court
South Street
Reading
RG1 4QS
UK

Ithaca Press is an imprint of Garnet Publishing Ltd.
www.ithacapress.co.uk

Copyright © The European Azerbaijan Society, 2011
www.teas.eu

All rights reserved.
No part of this book may be reproduced in any form or by
any electronic or mechanical means, including information
storage and retrieval systems, without permission in writing
from the publisher, except by a reviewer who may quote
brief passages in a review.

First Edition 2011

ISBN-13: 978-0-86372-390-2

British Library Cataloguing-in-Publication Data
A catalogue record for this book is available from the British Library

Cover photographs from English newspapers:
Illustrated London News, 16 September 1905; *The Sphere*, 30 September 1905
Frontispiece: Title page of *Qanli Iller*, M.S. Ordubadi, Baku, 1911

Design: Eldar Farzaliyev, Ismayil Mammadov

Printed in Lebanon by International Press:
interpress@int-press.com

Contents

Foreword..7
Our Purpose..15
Disclosure of the Causes..18
About the Tragic Events in Baku...............................25
Mournful Events in Nakhchivan................................33
Events in Irevan..41
Echmiadzin. The Events in Uchkilse..........................53
Events in Jabrail and Karyagin.................................57
Painful Events in Shusha, or the Wretchedness of Ignorance..............78
Second Tragedy in Shusha, or Goloshapov's Deception..................89
Sudden Onset of Tragedy in Baku..............................95
Scream of the Motherland..103
The Empty Illusions of the Armenians of Javanshir........................109
Painful Events in Ganja..126
Tragedies in Tiflis..136
Armenian-Muslim Clashes in Gazakh.........................141
Peace Negotiations in Tiflis.......................................146
Painful Events in Gatar..164
Events in Okhchu-Shabadak and Gapan Gorge..............173
Index..192

During the fair and happy reign of His Excellency Emperor Nicholas II,* ruler of Russia, Poland and Finland, disturbances took place in 1905 between the noble Muslim** and ancient Armenian nations. They added a page of grief and misfortune to the histories of these nations. This is a book about the recent events in the Caucasus.

Additional Note

This book, which is devoted to the recent revolutionary period in the Caucasus, is published and disseminated by Aga Murtuza Mukhtarov.*** I wish success to the Mukhtarovs in their deeds and desires, because they believe that this is of great historical importance. We hope that our people will not forget such Fathers of the Nation.

Mammad Said

---

* Tsar Nicholas II (1894-1917)

** Here and later throughout the text Muslims means Azerbaijanis.

*** Aga Murtuza Mukhtarov (1855-1920). Celebrated Azerbaijani entrepreneur and philanthropist.

Editorial note: starred footnotes are by the present editorial board.
numbered footnotes are by Ordubadi.

Foreword

Years of Blood: A History of the Armenian-Muslim Clashes in the Caucasus, 1905-1906 occupies a special niche in the literary life of Mammad Said Ordubadi (1872-1950), a celebrated Azerbaijani historical researcher and the author of a series of historical novels. Written with fresh impressions of familiar tragic events, this work was completed in 1908. However, it was published only in 1911, in the old Azerbaijani (Arabic) alphabet. After publication, the book attracted much attention, thanks to the abundant facts provided and the validity of its findings. It proved, however, not to correspond with official ideology and was thus not even mentioned in research dedicated to the writer's literary work. The book was published for the second time 80 years later, in 1990 - when the Nagorno-Karabagh conflict was at its height, unfolding as a result of territorial claims by Armenia and separatists, and secretly supported by the leadership of the USSR. Although some deletions were made for the new edition, the book again attracted a large readership.

Thus, *Years of Blood* has continuously been subject to censorship for its subject matter. Meanwhile it is, in the real sense of the words, a weighty work of research into the history of the Armenian-Muslim clashes of 1905 and 1906. The author set down the aim of his work, choice of structure and thematic frame as follows: "Anyway, I dare to pen the history, to present readers with this simple work, which will stamp an imprint of grief on any sign of humanity. To be more honest and open, by describing the tragedy which took place between these two nations, I want my compatriots to learn from the misfortunes of the past, and my book is a memorial to my compatriots, a book describing the screams of the motherland" Coming back to this same idea, the writer states later: "I hope that esteemed Muslim and Armenian writers will read this unbiased, perfect and true history with pure hearts, souls and consciences, review it as reformers and will not belittle Said." The author uses contemporary methods of analysis, which place the book within the ambit of modern historical-sociological research. In order to collect first hand data from original sources, a large number of correspondents were requested to provide written witness, from which Said assembled an overall flow of events. The author writes: "I sorted through 245 letters of correspondence sent to me and put them down on paper without changing their contents, simply adapting them to the style of the time and to my own style. Both Armenians and Muslims must know that I have not given any space in this book to scandal, to quarrels between those shepherds who are cursed by all, to my personal preferences, to thefts committed for personal gain, or to crimes. I have tried to describe accurately and without bias the events which took place for nationalist reasons, from nationalist motives; the victories and defeats of both sides, their injuries and their losses."

The other group of sources used for the book comprises materials from periodicals. As in the section on events in Irevan, the author takes care to declare the source of the information he uses for the given situation: "This chapter is based on letters sent to newspapers and magazines and collected by Mir Abbas Mir Bagirzade". A similar clarification anticipates the essay on Ganja: "Information about the events which began on 1 November 1905 was collected by Ali Akber bey Rafibeyov from a magazine in Russian and from other letters. I have compiled and translated them."

The author's wish to be objective, to observe authenticity of fact in everything is, perhaps, the book's main distinction.

One more quality distinguishes it from the publications of Armenian authors (See e.g. Alibekov I., *Yelizavetpolskie krovavie dni pered sudom obshestva*, Tiflis, 1906). It is that Mammad Said does not try "to exert pressure on" the reader's conclusion, preferring to give readers the opportunity to make their own judgment, based on the events described. Thus, preserving the fidelity of the scientific-cognitive weight of fact, the author does not neglect the scientific-ethical aspect in his research of such a complicated and delicate topic. The structure of the book allows the reader to track chronologically the reasons for the Armenian-Muslim clashes of 1905-1906, their development and the main problems and consequences.

Dwelling particularly upon the reasons for conflict, Mammad Said Ordubadi noted that "Our peoples speak of many reasons for the outbreak of events in the Caucasus." However, he then singles out four reasons, after mentioning that "I do not like to speak of ... unworthy things". First of all, he mentions the actions of the "Dashnaksutyun" party. "... the Armenian Dashnaksutyun Party has developed a despotic method of rule; this has resulted in a number of bloody acts of terror in the Caucasus. I do not think that the honest Armenian and Muslim will deny this. I have received 245 letters and over 400 pieces of information about the activity of the Dashnaksutyun Party, all of them are on my writing desk." A further reason was indicated, closely connected - "the Armenian desire for autonomy". The author thinks that this principal ambition is revealed in the territorial claims against Muslims and the practice of severe ethnic cleansing "to drive the Muslims out of their motherland and to build an Armenian state there". The third reason - "the indifference" of the local government authorities. According to the writer, "When the Great Russian war erupted, the central government was preoccupied with its own affairs and fate" as a result of which the "local authorities acted wilfully, doing nothing to quell the Armenian-Muslim disturbances." As an example he serves up "the provocative actions of such dishonest men" as the police chief of Nakhchivan, who only encouraged "the criminals to commit further crimes".

While writing about the reasons, Mammad Said mentions the ignorance and lack of all kinds of knowledge on the part of the Muslims of the Caucasus. In his opinion, uneducated Muslims, with limited understanding of political subtleties, had no inkling of the real positions of the local (not to mention senior!) Tsarist administration in the provinces, whereas the Armenians skilfully exploited this factor. Compounding this was a lack of military training (recruitment to the army) and a shortage of arms: the situation, then, becomes clear. The author writes, with good reason: "We must remember that the Armenians nudged their soldiers in Baku into testing the Muslims. If the Muslims had been vigilant, made preparations and punished the Armenians, the tragedies in the Caucasus would have been put to an end; the Armenians would have been made aware of the natural courage and bravery of the Muslims. In the initial tragedies the Armenians did not have enough soldiers..."

Years of Blood could be called a historical-geographical essay on the Armenian-Muslim clashes of 1905-1906. Let's take a look at the chapter headings in the book: *About the Tragic Events in Baku*; *Echmiadzin. The Events in Uchkilse*; *Events in Jabrail and Karyagin* etc. They comprise almost a protocol description of events in those places.

Any conflict, one way or another, ends in a peace as a result of negotiation. In this respect, the chapter *Peace Negotiations in Tiflis* attracts special interest. Ordubadi informs his readers about the dramatic atmosphere in which extended negotiations were held. Compared with other publications (See e.g. Mayevski V.F. *Armyano-tatarskaya smuta na Kavkaze, kak odin iz fazisov armyanskoqo voprosa.* Tiflis, 1915) this chapter includes new facts from the records of the debates. The writer draws a conclusion from the course of the debates which is difficult to dispute: "The Armenians' participation in the assembly was not dictated by a desire to achieve peace, but to defeat the Muslims in a battle of words in the presence of government officials and, later, to ask for further benefits and compensation for damage". The book comes to an end, but without conclusion or, at least, without concluding remarks. And it is quite clear that the author wants readers to make up their own minds.

Ordubadi's book is one of the main sources on the Armenian-Muslim conflicts of 1905-1906. It is no coincidence that, following the publication of its second edition (1990), it became a commonly quoted source in contemporary publications, including those written abroad.

There is one more quite important aspect: at the very beginning of his book, Ordubadi wrote: "Along with the Russian and Caucasian press, European and American publications speak heatedly and exhibit the closest interest in these events and their causes. We should also know that the articles published in the foreign press are full of contradictions and differences."

With a sense of regret, it should be noted that not much has changed since then. Therefore, to return to the history, to appreciate the facts anew, to develop a considered opinion about past events is of great scientific-cognitive importance, and this is why we present to a wider readership the first translation of Ordubadi's work into English.

Tale Heydarov
Founder and chairman of
The European Azerbaijan Society

YEARS OF BLOOD

A History of the Armenian-Muslim Clashes
in the Caucasus, 1905-1906

Our Purpose

When I take up my pen to put this history onto paper, recollections of grief and misfortune fill my heart. This is surprising. My pen is eager to describe the tragedies which suddenly burst forth in those blood-filled years; my conscience also betrays an extraordinary desire to execute this noble objective. My concern for the weakness of my emotions arises from the things I have witnessed: the cries for help rising to the heavens, the moral and material deprivation of the wretched people I have seen, the lack of hope for any improvement in a critical situation, and the latter's continuation.

Anyway, I dare to pen the history, to present readers with this simple work, which will stamp an imprint of grief on any sign of humanity. To be more honest and open, by describing the tragedy which took place between these two nations, I want my compatriots to learn from the misfortunes of the past, and my book is a memorial to my compatriots, a book describing the screams of the motherland. With God's help I have finished this book on which I worked, and for which I collected materials, for two years.* A thousand thanks to God that I was able to overcome the weakness of my emotions and that I raised my honour and worthiness to higher levels; of this I am proud. This is because I undertook an obligation to fulfil a task which is very important and necessary for my nation and, thank God, I fulfilled this noble task impeccably, by telling the truth. My spirit was not enough to achieve this noble and praiseworthy status. Besides, my pen and my strength lacked the ability, the skill to complete this important task. I was lifted to this level by the patriotism of the reporters and correspondents! I want all the nations of the Caucasus, be they Armenian or Muslim, to know that this historical essay is not by any means written from any personal

---

*The book was mainly completed in 1908.

or national hostility or bias, I have tried to describe all the tragedies and events in every location and to present them to readers in full and as they actually occurred. I sorted through 245 letters of correspondence sent to me and put them down on paper without changing their contents, simply adapting them to the style of the time and to my own style. Both Armenians and Muslims must know that I have not given any space in this book to scandal, to quarrels between those shepherds who are cursed by all, to my personal preferences, to thefts committed for personal gain, or to crimes. I have tried to describe accurately and without bias the events which took place for nationalist reasons, from nationalist motives; the victories and defeats of both sides, their injuries and their losses. Everyone should also be aware that I appealed to local reporters through the *Irshad*[1] and *Teze heyat*[2] newspapers to convey unbiased and true information. I also sent letters to reporters and penmen, asking them to inform me about the behaviour of the belligerent parties when the riots took place. I am proud that I received letters clear of any personal bias or provocation, and I published them (May God bless you all). I hope that esteemed Muslim and Armenian writers will read this unbiased, perfect and true history with pure hearts, souls and consciences, review it as reformers and will not belittle Said.[*] In fact, I am not a writer. My penmanship may be compared to a particle relative to the sun which illuminates the whole Universe. The nations of the Caucasus should also know this: by writing this book my goal is not to clear my nation of responsibility, to present it as a humane nation and to hold Armenians responsible for the grave events, to describe them as brutal, inhumane creatures. Then what is my goal? My goal is to write about the errors, misdeeds and crimes of Armenians and Muslims in those two years…Perhaps after reading this book both

---

[1] *Irshad* - a daily socio-political and literary newspaper, published in Baku, in Azerbaijani (17 December 1905-25 June 1908). Its editor was A. Agayev.

[2] *Teze heyat* - a daily socio-political, economic and literary newspaper, published in Baku in the *Kaspiy* printing-house (7 April 1907- 7 October 1908). Its editor was Hashim bey Vezirov, publisher Haji Zeynalabdin Taghiyev.

[*] i. e. the author

parties will feel some degree of regret and shame in the future. Readers must also understand that my goal is also to tell Muslims that they suffered these misfortunes because of their ignorance, lack of knowledge and science, as well as to tell Armenians that they have been the victims of the illusions and empty, injurious dreams of some of their writers. We must also know that although this book is full of events and is devoted to the tragic events of the past two years, still it may benefit both nations morally and spiritually. I hope that esteemed Armenian writers will translate this unbiased book into Russian, or Armenian, to allow both nations to understand their mistakes and misdeeds, and leave it as a bouquet of flowers for revival. It may allow those writers who have ideas of instigating crimes through their works, to abstain. After all that has been said, I think it is necessary for me to write about the reasons for the outbreak of the fighting, to pour the cool water of love and brotherhood over people's feelings and over the dreams of both nations that burn with the desire for revenge.

Along with the Russian and Caucasian press, European and American publications speak heatedly and exhibit the closest interest in these events and their causes. We should also know that the articles published in the foreign press are full of contradictions and differences. Although it is necessary to say which of them is true and which a lie, yet we abstain from doing so because of a lack of time and space, it will suffice to deal with four important factors which led to the events under discussion. I shall try to describe them in succession.

Disclosure of the Causes

Our peoples speak of many reasons for the outbreak of events in the Caucasus. As mentioned above, there is a lot of controversial information in the press. But we do not have the opportunity to write about all of this, because it contradicts my determination not to renew old griefs, and I do not like to speak of such unworthy things. To my mind, and as I understand it, these riots had four causes, and I shall try to reveal them.

The first was that the Armenian Dashnaksutyun* Party has developed a despotic method of rule; this has resulted in a number of bloody acts of terror in the Caucasus. I do not think that the honest Armenian and Muslim will deny this. I have received 245 letters and over 400 pieces of information about the activity of the Dashnaksutyun Party, all of them are on my writing desk. I do not have space for so much painful and heartrending detail in the pages of this book; quotations from some of them must suffice.

1. Before the clashes in Ganja on 18 November 1905, members of Dashnaksutyun had murdered an innocent villager of Bahmanli (on 8 November) to provoke the Muslims into fighting.

2. They killed a poor Iranian** in Ganja.

3. In Ganja, in the Armenian quarter called Gosha Chinar, members of Dashnaksutyun rained bullets onto the residents of the village of Mollajelilli.

4. On 12 November they murdered a Muslim in Amos Perov's mill.

5. The telegram from Governor General Levitsky of the Gazakh

---

* *Dashnaksutyun* (Union) Armenian nationalist party. Founded in 1890 in Tiflis. The main organization behind the Armenian-Azerbaijani conflicts of 1905-1906.

** They were incomers from South (Iranian) Azerbaijan.

district, addressed to Viceroy Count Vorontsov-Dashkov,* which was published in the *Kaspiy*³ newspaper on 9 March (№54). I hope that everybody has read or heard about this. It is about the crimes committed by the Dashnaksutyun.

6. After the events in Ganja, the Armenian Gnchakist⁴ committee proposed reconciliation and peace, but this was violated by the Dashnaksutyun; the Armenians confirm it themselves. We shall speak about this in detail when we come to the events in Ganja.

7. Several days before the tragedy in Nakhchivan, a Muslim was martyred by members of Dashnaksutyun while he was praying.** In a word, the Dashnaks committed many crimes in Shusha, Baku, Jabrail and Javanshir, as well as in the district of Zengezur. I do not think that it is necessary to list them here, because they will all be described in chronological order in this book.

Besides, we think that the roles played by the commanders of the Dashnaksutyun, namely Hamazasp, Aram, Bedo, men like Agabey, Bagrat, Sograt and others, will prove how bloodthirsty they are.

The second cause was the indifference of the local authorities when fighting started. When the Great Russian war*** erupted, the central government was preoccupied with its own affairs and fate, the low level, local authorities acted wilfully, doing nothing to quell the Armenian-Muslim disturbances. If they ever did anything, they supported one party, but acted dishonestly towards the other out of fear of Armenian terrorism. It is possible to say that they sup-

---

* I.I. Vorontsov-Dashkov (1837-1916), Deputy from the Caucasus, 1905-1915.

³ *Kaspiy*-a socio-political and literary newspaper published in Russian in Baku from January 1881 to March 1919, financed by the great Azerbaijani philanthropist Haji Zeynalabdin Taghiyev.

⁴ Gnchak (Gnchak) - a small Armenian bourgeois party founded in 1887 by a group of Armenian students in Geneva. It had its own publication of the same name. After the revolution of 1905-1907 it became nationalist and reactionary. Then it assumed the name of "Socialist-Democratic Party" in order to attract the masses, but as it did great harm to the workers' movement, it lost its reputation and, after the establishment of Soviet power, migrated to the United States.

** namaz, Arabic, salyat (prayer). Muslim prayers - five-times daily.

*** The revolution of 1905-1907.

pressed one party and compelled the other to seek revenge. Thus were the most beautiful towns of the Caucasus burnt and destroyed; our homes were turned into pools of blood. The proof lies in the provocative actions of such dishonest men as Angil, police chief of the Nakhchivan district. He not only failed to extinguish what was burning but, on the contrary, he added fuel to the fire, inciting the criminals to commit further crimes.

There is no need to explain this, because it has been discussed in detail in relation to the events in Nakhchivan. I think that to hide the facts is detrimental to the futures of both nations. As a result of the damnable actions of men like police chief Angil, the Armenians suffered the wrath of the Muslims and were defeated. They were defeated, but then Cossack commanders, men like Krylov, acted in concert with the Armenians, set fire to the shops of Muslims, burned their goods and deprived them of their property.

If we hide such things, it will be to earn the damnation of our Prophet, and God Almighty would also not be pleased. I think, besides, there is ample proof of my words in what I say about the actions of General Goloshapov in Shusha. In brief, it takes time to put all of this onto paper; I believe readers will bear this in mind.

The third cause of the disturbances was a lack of knowledge and education, and the Muslims' ignorance of ongoing processes and events.* The Muslims are ignorant of science and politics, thus they did not think about the mindset of Russian officials in the Caucasus and did not think about how the Armenians were using it. After the tragedy in Baku, Armenian-Muslim relations remained tense for so long because of the Muslims' ignorance. Another cause was the fact that the Muslims were unarmed and unaware of current world affairs. We must remember that the Armenians nudged their soldiers in Baku into testing the Muslims. If the Muslims had been vigilant, made preparations and punished the Armenians, the tragedies in the Caucasus would have been put to an end; the

---

*The Tsarist Government carried out a strict colonial policy with regard to Muslims. The Empire provided no relevant education or media for them. They were practically deprived of access to information about events.

Armenians would have been made aware of the natural courage and bravery of the Muslims. In the initial tragedies the Armenians did not have enough soldiers to occupy all the Caucasus. They wanted to crush the Muslim forces by ruses and politics, and with the help of a handful of volunteer soldiers. So they made peace in Baku and silenced and pacified the Muslims in order to begin the war in Shusha, then they made peace in Shusha and started to burn and destroy other places in Ganja province.* The Muslims were at first unaware of such things, but later, by the time they understood the cunning of the Armenians, the latter were mobilizing Armenian soldiers from Iran and Turkey to crush the Muslims here.

Two Armenian corpses found on the battlefield of Okhchu-Shabadak provide sufficient proof; letters found in their pockets showed that one was from Turkey, the other from Iran. Well, let me reiterate my main point: the ignorance of the Muslims was the third cause of these disturbances and murders.

The fourth cause was the Armenian desire for autonomy. There is no need for my pen to exert itself to prove this. The Armenians' monthly visits to London, Paris and Northern USA and their negotiations there are the evidence. Following a programme developed by the English, the Armenians worked hard and long for autonomy in Turkey. Finally, after the slaughters in Sasun and Zeytun and the tragedy in Van, they once more appealed to England, and what they heard from the English was this: "The British navy is helpless in a war waged in the mountains of Turkey's Anatolia. What can we do?" This discouraged the Armenians somewhat in their drive for autonomy in Turkey. Failing in England, they were obliged to send Catholicos Mkrtych to Berlin**, that is, to Germany this time. In Germany Mkrtych received the order from Germany that "now it is

---

* Officially - Elizavetpol Province. Established in 1867. In the early 20th century the following districts were within the province: Elizavetpol, Aresh, Jabrail (Karyagin), Javanshir, Zengezur, Kazakh, Nukha and Shusha.

** The Berlin Congress was held (June 1878) following the Russian-Turkish war of 1877-1878. An Armenian delegation participated in the Congress. Spiritual leader Mkrtych Khrimyan (1820-1907) was included in the delegation. The mission came to grief.

time for war, time for the sword", and Mkrtych conveyed this to the Armenians, who immediately began organizing the Dashnaksutyun Party in Turkey; they controlled its activity there. The Turkish government stared in wonder and began to monitor these processes, Catholicos Mkrtych was exiled from Istanbul to Holy Jerusalem[*] and Dashnaksutyun activity was severely restricted (because much was said about the work of this party in the Tiflis peace negations between Armenians and Muslims). When they saw that Turkey viewed their new party less enthusiastically, they turned their eyes to the Caucasus, dreaming of the revival of the Armenia[**] which had been abolished by the Bizhans[5] of Iran in ancient times. Proof of this is that in 1878, at the siege of Kars, the Armenian Colonel Loris-Melikov[***] demanded that the government hand over the ruins of Ani,[6] near Echmiadzin; this was a hopeless pipedream. The initiator and inspirer of this illusion was the Armenian writer Artsruni.[****] This so-called writer saw that the situation in Turkey was not favourable to such a project, it would be too difficult to realize his dream, thus he advised the Armenians to move to the Caucasus.[*****] Following this migration Artsruni died, but he handed

---

[*] Jerusalem.

[**] Ancient Armenia was outside the Caucasus. Armenia was divided between Rome and the Sasanids pursuant to a treaty signed in 387, after which Armenia practically ceased to exist.

[5] Bizhan - name of one of the athletes in the poem *Shah-nameh* by Firdousi, a Persian poet. The writer wants to say that they were driven away by the brave sons of Iran.

[***] Loris - M.T. Melikov (1825 - 1892), cavalry general from 1875. Using his military position during the Russian-Turkish war of 1877-1878, he had a policy of strengthening Armenian positions in occupied provinces of the Ottoman Empire such as Kars, Ardagan etc.

[6] Ruins of Ani - said to be an Armenian administrative centre in Turkey. Melikov dreamed of the restoration of the ancient Armenian government.

[****] G. Artsruni (1845-1892), Armenian publicist, editor-in-chief of the newspaper *Mshak* from 1872 until his death. An ideologist behind militant Armenian nationalism.

[*****] The history of Armenian migration to the Caucasus is linked to Tsar Peter I (1683-1725). This policy was subsequently continued by his successors. Following the Turkmenchay treaty (1828) Armenian migration to the Caucasus, in particular to the lands of Azerbaijan, became a mass movement.

on his mission to Bahadurov,* a member of the former State Duma of Russia. This man continued to pursue Artsruni's dreams and instructions after the latter's death. Finally he managed to instigate the Armenian-Muslim slaughter and become a member of the State Duma of Russia. When leaving for Petersburg, he wanted to take Artsruni's instructions and read them to the Duma. To put an end to the Armenian-Muslim clashes he suggested giving the province of Baku and the lowlands of Ganja province to the Muslims, leaving the highlands and mountainous territories of Karabagh, as well as the province of Irevan, for the Armenians, merging them with the plain of Kars to thus build an Armenian state. It is also evidence of their long-extant dream that they spread a rumour that the Russians would enlist the youth of Kars Sanjaks** into the army, thus frightening the Muslims into moving to other parts of Turkey. They also advised Shia Muslims in the Caucasus to move to Iran. In short, the Armenians prepared and were very active in pursuit of their national goal. Following their next initiative they made preparations for the tragedy in Baku. To fulfil Artsruni's behests, they aimed to drive the Muslims out of their motherland and to build an Armenian state there. It becomes evident from the above that the fourth cause of the disturbances was connected to Armenian pipedreams about autonomy.

Let the spirit of Mr. Artsruni not be offended, although he is a writer of the past, still his influence on humble men like us is very important, perhaps even necessary.

Let his pure spirit rejoice!

Mammad Said

---

* Kh. Bahadurov, Deputy to the 1st State Duma (20 February - 9 June 1906), cadet.

** Sanjaks - territorial /administrative unit in the Ottoman Empire.

About the Tragic Events in Baku

On the tragic events in Baku which suddenly erupted on 6 February 1905, and which form a page of deep regret in the history of both nations.

Disclosure of the purpose. As we described at the beginning, the Armenians indulged their illusions, committed various provocations and rioted against the Muslims. They oppressed the Muslims at every opportunity, abusing them with bitter words and treating them unkindly in ways detrimental to their dignity. The Muslims knew what the outcome would be, took defensive precautions and never relaxed their vigilance. But the local government was only concerned with petty crimes and was far from capable of dealing with such major events. It became clear that the two nations, which had already broken off friendly relations, were given licence to confront each other. In those days the Armenians had already begun to oppress the Muslims. Some of the Armenian population did not approve of the disturbances, but the most powerful and influential section thought it would be better to begin at once, not to leave it for another day. These people represented the Armenian parties and their words had some influence among their people. It began as expected.

On 2 February a Muslim by the name of Agarza was killed by activists of the Armenian Committee in Kubinka.* When a tragedy like this occurred, the Muslims felt offended, because their national dignity had been insulted. Imagine! Could anyone restrain the Muslim volunteers?! They were confused and aggrieved, but the Muslim women did not demand revenge. Then an Armenian soldier

---
*The names of old and relevant new streets, squares and blocks in Baku are included in the index.

killed an innocent Muslim while taking him in for interrogation. This increased the Muslims' fury. This was on 6 February, the day on which Baku became a river of blood. This was the day on which the Armenians wanted to begin the disturbances, but the Muslims were perplexed. These two friendly neighbours became eager to kill each other within moments; they broke off relations and became circumspect with each other. Finally, the artificial bomb of riot, primed over the course of many years, exploded and set fire to the whole Caucasus. Was this really a bombshell? Yes, the bombshell was the tragedy that took place in Baku on 6 February, it cocked guns across the Caucasus. On that day riots and disturbances were expected to break out everywhere, in every corner of Baku. When information about the murder of a Muslim by the name of Babayev reached the Muslims, they rose openly to fight and attacked the Armenians. The factions began to exchange fire in the area of the city called Quarter Four. The skirmishing was astonishingly fierce. The Armenians maintained heavy firing. Half an hour after the murder of the aforementioned Babayev, Artem Shinkov, a conductor on a horse-tram, was killed in Vorontsovskaya Street, then an unknown Russian was killed by unknown men and left in a pool of his own blood on the corner of Tsitsianovskaya and Chadrovaya streets. After the murders of these men, serious skirmishing began in all quarters of the city, both sides maintaining continuous fire. Throughout that day and night there were explosions and much destruction in the city. Shooting was heard until dawn; in the morning 13 men were found dead on the streets and their bodies were taken to hospitals. On 7 February skirmishing resumed; the Armenians launched fullscale riots and so the Muslims were obliged to take to arms. They fought with pistols and rifles, as in real battles. The Armenians could not withstand the attacks of the Muslims, took to their heels and found sanctuary inside their houses. They continued to fire at Muslims and passers-by from their windows and roofs, paying no heed to the nationality or sex of their targets. The fighting was fiercest in the quarter where the Krasilnikovs lived, near the Hotel Madrid, on the corner of

Bazarnaya and Guberniskaya streets. In the quarter where Amilov and Korsakov lived and where there was also a bathhouse, the Muslims met resistance. Passers-by were also fired on indiscriminately from the upper floors of Haji Zeynalabdin Taghiyev's house. Rioting spread to all plants and factories in Baku. The populations mixed and became entangled; arms were discharged in all directions. Women ran through the streets hand-in-hand with their children, found no haven, stood helpless and confused and did not know where to go. Battles raged in Balakhani, an oil producing field, derricks were set on fire. Muslims who were humane and understood the root of the problem were sheltering and rescuing Armenians. On that day about 40 Armenian bodies were collected from the streets. The Muslims took in their wounded and dead. Many Muslim shops were looted and houses burnt as a result of the disturbances. Of the Armenians, shops belonging to Minas Simonov, Mugdusi Ohanesyan, the Ayrapetyans Brothers and others were looted. The police did not have the means to stop the looting of these shops, to protect them. That is, it was impossible for them to prevent the plunder, because the perpetrators were mainly Muslim workers from Iran, emigrant Dashnaksutyun Armenians and other volunteers from Turkey. On 7 February, as the battle raged, 20 Cossacks, divided into two teams, began to move along the streets, one of the teams took up a position in Shamakinsky, the other in the Bazaar. When the skirmishing intensified, the local police chiefs, helpless and lacking the means to fulfil their duties, demanded help from the Cossacks, but got none. They were told: "There are few of us, we cannot do anything". By about 12 o'clock in the morning, the situation in the city was critical. Young Muslim volunteers fought bravely against the Armenians and their regular soldiers. As for the leading Muslims, they tried to shelter and rescue Armenians as best they could. At this point the government sent soldiers to each side, each team being ten in number. But it was an empty gesture. To separate tens of thousands of battling people it was necessary to send not ten, but thousands of soldiers, and very competent, trained soldiers. Lt. Colonel Kuzminsky, commander of the Salyan Regiment was instructed to restore order; he then appeared in the street with 12 soldiers, to the sound of trumpets and drums. The warring parties dispersed a little, but when the soldiers moved on the looting and slaughter were resumed. The district police officer went personally to the Lt. Colonel and asked him to order his soldiers to shoot into the air in order to frighten and scatter people, but he got the answer: "This is not your affair, we know our own duty well and we fulfil it". There is little doubt that men like this district police-officer, men who occupied official posts in these areas where the battle was fiercest, would quit their posts and leave if they received such replies. And so it happened. It is clear that these two hostile nations were left to each other's mercy. But we must also say that the Muslims were not so ruthless; they saved and protected Armenians everywhere they could, they sheltered and fed them in their own houses. The battle continued fiercely in Krasnavodskaya and Surakhanskaya streets, at the corner of the church in Bolshaya Morskaya Street. The Muslims rescued many Armenians from this street, including at House 195, where Akim Isayevich and his family found shelter and food, remaining safe from looting and slaughter. Their protectors were the Muslims Agakishi Aliyev and his brother Huseyngulu Karbalayi Abdulla oglu. The Armenians themselves have written a letter about this and their rescuers. The letter is signed by the Armenians Mikail Artemyans, Babajanov and Sarkis Minayevich Ovanesov. One of the fighting hot spots was the area around Molokan Gardens.

Agadadash Veliyev hid Arshak Durniyans and his two children - grammar school pupils - in his house. That Armenian family had initially been hidden by their neighbours, Huseyngulu Mahmudov and Meshedi Hanifa Jafarov.

Many Armenians were rescued there, too. It should also be noted that the unmarried and widowed Muslim women in that quarter resisted the looters and saved the property and the lives of Armenians. There is a letter from Arshak Durniyans about this which is full of gratitude. The letter is dated 19 February 1905.

In those tragic days, which began on 6 February, Stepan

Avetisov, the Arzumanov family and others found sanctuary in the houses of Muslims. We mentioned the name of Agarza Babayev above. He was killed by Armenians at the beginning of the disturbances. But his nephew won the respect of the public for his mercy and compassion. Although his uncle had been ruthlessly slaughtered by Armenians, he saved the lives of his enemies and protected them. He fed all the members of Davud Oganesov's family and his tenants, and saved them from looting and slaughter. Long live my merciful brothers! Glory to them, because they spread the fame and might of Islam! But the Armenians were engaged in the slaughter of poor, humble Muslims in the street who did not know where to hide. The Muslim women trembled with fear and sometimes even forgot about their children. Nevertheless, these kind-hearted, merciful women joined their husbands and saved their Armenian neighbours, with whom they had lived side by side for many years. Evidence of this is the fact that three Muslim women saved 50 Armenians and fed them all for four days. A letter of gratitude is signed by an Armenian named Garakhanyan, I have it on my writing desk. Long live our honest and merciful mothers. May they live long and bring up merciful children. On the night of 8 February, Baku, full of glory and deprivation, became a living hell; bombs were exploding and the oil magnates' mansions were burning; they resembled erupting volcanoes. The security detachments were removed and the town was left unprotected. It was left to the disposal of the looters and the ghosts of those who had returned to Baku after witnessing the slaughter of their innocent offspring; they desired to return to their abode and rained curses down upon us. The barbarians took to looting and murder, and burned and destroyed many enterprises and factories. The main pogroms and destruction took place in the streets of Tsitsianovskaya and Guberniskaya, both sides suffering great damage. On 8 February the slaughter and looting continued. Goods taken from the shop belonging to Mirza Aramyans were retrieved from the looters and transported by cart to the police station for protection. At about ten o'clock looters attacked the Aslanovs' house and three or four houses nearby in order to destroy and pillage, but security guards protected the houses and repelled the attack. On the corner of these streets and on the Boulevard, looting was as fierce as ever. When night fell, there were attempts to set fire to looted houses, but the police extinguished them. At this time the house of a Muslim was tragically looted and burned in Surakhanskaya Street. The house was attacked by a crowd of Armenians and it was pillaged. This was reported by a police officer serving in Quarter Four. In this quarter the Armenians subjected the Muslims to heavy and ceaseless bombardment. Nobody could have withstood such a situation. The troops who arrived there to stop the bombardment could not hold out under the shooting and were obliged to retreat.

Two more poor Muslims were murdered when firing intensified from both sides.

It was disclosed that there was a house full of Armenians engaged in murder and pillage. The police officer responsible for that quarter conveyed the information to the relevant bodies in the town.

In this quarter the Armenians were bombarding the Muslims intensively. Nobody could endure such a situation. It was the same with the troops; unable to hold out, they took to their heels and retreated.

As the exchange of fire grew fiercer, two poor Muslims were ruthlessly killed. The police, with the support of the chief of the city police, asked for a detachment of the Dagestan Regiment and a firefighting team to help. The firefighters were not very willing to act and so the police officer in charge of Quarter Four took a team of soldiers and made his way towards Aslanov's house. When they were at the threshold, unknown people opened fire on the house. The police officer, not taking any undue risks, was obliged to return with the soldiers to their location. Again night fell and the property of both Muslims and Armenians, without distinction, was looted and set on fire. The situation in Baku on that day was so critical, confused and dangerous that it became impossible to pick up the wounded and bodies from the streets and transport them to hospitals because of the shelling and the burning mansions.

In this way slaughter and fire spread to all parts of Baku, and it continued relentlessly until 10 February; countless crimes were committed. Rioting and fires raged in the oil refineries of Balakhani. The Armenians willingly joined the riots in Balakhani and there were many Muslim workers eager to take part in the looting and slaughter. But the Muslim elders obstructed the rioters and protected Armenians and workers from other nationalities.

We have received many letters highly appreciative of the mercy shown by the Muslims. This is confirmed by a letter sent by the workers of the Reno Company. They also list the names of those who protected them. They were Haji Najafgulu Ibrahimov, Aga Sultanali Hashimov, Abdulali Babayev, the Hajiyev brothers, Meshedi Gulu Agamuhammad oglu, Meshedi Aghahuseyn Molla Hasan oglu, Haji Fatali Aghali oglu and others mentioned in the letter. The letter is signed by workers of the Reno Company. According to the information at our disposal, if Muslims had not protected and saved Armenians in Baku, perhaps about 3000 would have been killed.

The disturbances continued fiercely from 6 February to 10 February. The human losses on both sides were no more than 1,000, but the cost in damage to property exceeded millions of manats. Although the government made efforts to quell the conflict, it could not do anything substantial; everybody knows this. I can describe the tragic events in Baku in this book, but do not do so in order to leave the two nations unaware of the brutalities committed.

It is clear from the information above that the Armenians were completely defeated in Baku and doomed to misfortune. On the other hand, it is highly surprising that after such preparation before the events, after such effort, the Armenians were defeated. I think that the Armenians were themselves guilty of their own defeat because, before the fighting broke out, they allowed the Muslims to become aware of their intentions. Being aware of the Armenians' plans, the Muslims took measures to ensure their own security. Had the Armenians caught the Muslims unawares with their attacks, then the latter would have losses not in the thousands, but in the tens of thousands. It is also necessary to say that the Muslims of Baku did not take a serious part in the rioting; they simply took security precautions. There are many letters to support this. But as we have mentioned some of them above, we do not think it necessary to cite them again. We hope that hence these two nations will dream of nothing but love and devotion to each other.

I must also say that the two nations will not dream of taking revenge, they will live in peace as before, restoring their former friendly relations and engaging in the defence of their own rights.

Finally, I ask readers to read the events I describe here attentively and pardon me for the mistakes they encounter in the book.

Mammad Said Ordubadi

Mournful Events in Nakhchivan

Following the Armenian-Muslim confrontation in Baku, in Nakhchivan, by the beginning of May 1905, the Armenian and Muslim populations were living in constant alarm and agitation. But the Armenian population did not show their fear and continued to trouble the Muslims as before. There were rumours in the town that the Armenians had plenty of firearms and would subject the Muslims to sudden attacks. This was expected at any moment. When one analyzes the policy pursued by the Armenians, there is nothing surprising. They thought that there was no nation superior to them in the Caucasus. Thus they were trying to distribute firearms and other weapons to all locations populated by Armenians. The residents of Nakhchivan could not leave their houses at night and in the daytime they could not go too far from their property, out of fear. Nakhchivan was surrounded by Armenian villages on all sides, they were able to call on as many Armenian soldiers from Irevan (Yerevan) as they wanted and, consequently, they behaved quite brutally towards the Muslims and addressed them only in derogatory terms.

The town of Nakhchivan is located in a significant position within the province of Sisiyan; it was possible for the Armenians to assemble as many soldiers there as they wanted and at any time. They also had many members of their national parties there. The Armenian soldiers were always looking for a pretext to involve the Muslims in a fight. Thus on 5 May, at about 3 o'clock in the afternoon, three Muslim residents of the village of Jahri were mortally wounded while passing the Armenian village of Shykhmahmud. When the news reached Nakhchivan, its residents were agitated and troubled. On the same day the Armenians closed their shops and went home, or assembled in the church. The reason remained unknown to the Muslims. The situation continued like this until 7 May, when a Muslim was murdered while passing the village of Tunbul (Tunbul is a village inhabited by both Muslims and Armenians, one-third being Armenians, two-third Muslims). Now think about the preparations they had made. Being in the minority, they were planning victory over the Muslims in the village.

As for the Muslims, they were frightened and did not know what to do. On 8 May Baranovsky, the Vice-Governor of Irevan;* Agamalov, the head of the town and Jafargulu Khan Nakhchivanskiy, who had been in Petersburg a month before, came to Nakhchivan. Having heard about the arrival of these high level officials, the Muslim inhabitants crowded round their door and began to complain about the misdeeds of the Armenians. At first they complained thus: "For what the Armenians have done, we forgive them; let bygones be bygones, let them return to the bazaar and resume trading". On 9 May, the Muslim residents of Jahri came to the governor and complained: "The roads to our village have been blocked on all sides by the Armenians. We earnestly request that the government ensures the security of the roads". In this way and manner, Muslims came from all corners of Nakhchivan with their complaints. Unfortunately, all the complaints remained unanswered and the plaintiffs were disappointed. The Armenians began to offend the Muslims by every means and in all manners; cursing and insulting them. On the night of 9 May of the same year, a resident of Nakhchivan by the name of Ali Haji Bayramzade was shot by residents of the Armenian village of Aliabad, by the spring in the field: his body was riddled with seven bullets. News of the murder sparked real terror in the town. On 11May, a rich man from the Armenian village of Gultepe was killed, together with members of his family, by so-called Armenian patriots. The Armenians accused the Muslims of the crime. But the final investigation of the case revealed that the man and his family had been punished by members of the aforementioned Armenian parties. The name of the mur-

---

*The Vice-Governor of the Province is referred to here. Lt. Col V.P.Baranovsky was Vice-Governor of the Province from 1904-1913.

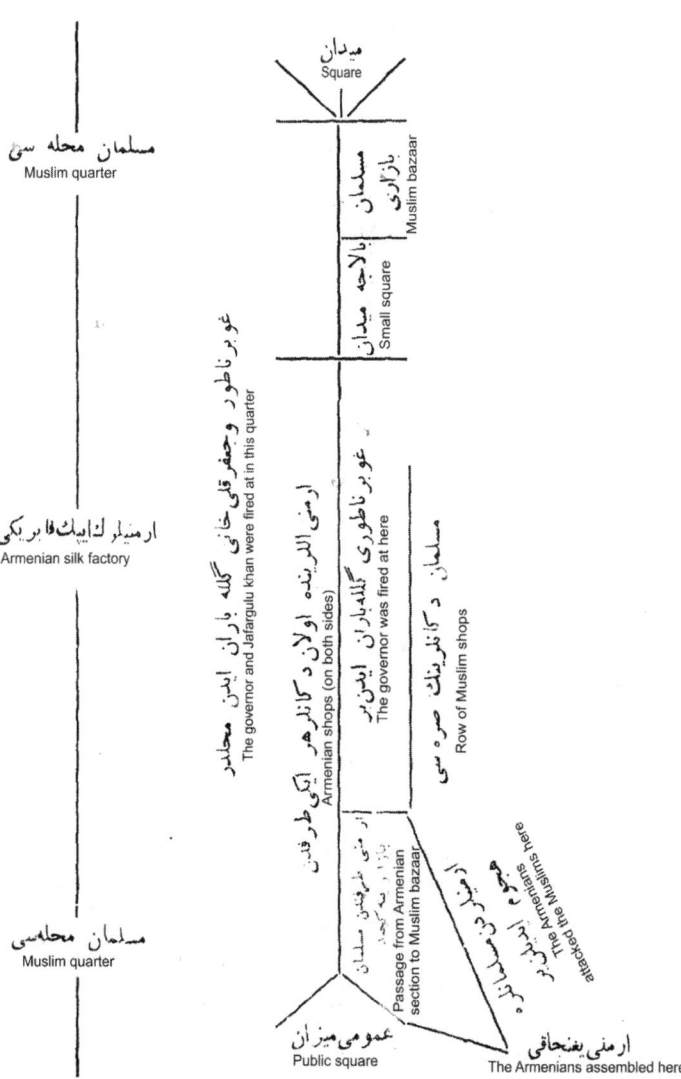

Plan of the quarter where the skirmish took place

dered Armenian was Khachatur. Later the same day, Vice-Governor Baranovsky confiscated several bombs from an Armenian whom he met when he was out riding on horseback. On the same night, that is, on 11 May, Armenians began to fire their guns in all parts of the town. Within two and a half hours there was nothing in the town but the sound of rifles, fire and smoke. The Muslims did not sustain any losses on that night, but it was impossible that the Armenians did not have any losses. Nevertheless, even if they had losses, they hid them, as they always did. That was a terrible night. Nobody, neither the aged nor the young, even small children, could sleep that night. Bullets cracked like lightning across windows and did not let babies sleep in their cradles. Everyone was wrapped in his own thoughts. A strong wind blew outside. A never-ending stream of bullets banged against the walls. The Muslims spent the night in troubled thought; their beds seemed to be a hell in which they writhed like snakes the whole night. It is true. The next morning, that is, on 12 May, they went to complain to the vice-governor. They told him about the night-time shootings and demanded that he take measures. In reply he said: "If they fire at you, catch them and take their pistols". Then, saying "I don't know, I can't do anything", the vice-governor drove the plaintiffs away. Even in this situation no enraged Armenian or disappointed and perplexed Muslim was found to ask him: "Mr. Governor, why then did you come here?" On that day the town and its outskirts were dangerous and so the inhabitants of Nakhchivan and the Iranian workers remained inside the town and bazaar. Following the governor's advice, the Iranian workers began to confiscate firearms from the Armenians. At ten o'clock a group of Armenian fedayeen approached the entrance of the bazaar and began to fire at the Muslims. Unaware of these events, the vice-governor, Jafargulu Khan; the head of the town, Agamalov; the head of Irevan and the police officer in charge, Mehdi khan Ordubadsky, arrived to investigate the sound of shooting. As their road lay through the bazaar, they were witnesses of the skirmish. They were fired on from several Armenian shops, opened that day by order of the governor himself. At that moment rifles opened fire from

Muslim shops close to the Armenian ones. The skirmish continued for two hours. During this battle the famous Armenian merchant Agamalov, along with his apprentices, the Khalatovs and others were murdered. Adamov's shop burned out completely, cause unknown. Five Muslims died and several people were wounded in the skirmish. The majority of Armenian shops and ten Muslim shops were looted. As the skirmish continued, chief of police Angil did nothing to prevent the murders, on the contrary, he encouraged the Armenian volunteers, saying "Be quick, my son, fire, my son, be quick". And when the looting began, he again encouraged the looters by saying "Hurry, take it away". In this way he incited the volunteers to crime. The looting and skirmishing lasted two hours, then both sides retreated to their houses. The governor was an eyewitness to everything that happened there. The night that followed was terrible, everybody sat at home. At 12 o'clock the sound of fierce shooting was heard from the Armenian quarter, then it grew and thundered across the whole town. The firing was mainly in that part of the town where the Armenian silk factories were located.

The night-time shootings were silenced by the governor. Finally, the Armenians ceased firing. News of the night's events caused fear and terror in the early morning. Looting and killing broke out everywhere. The villagers of Jahri were first to start; the residents of this village consisted equally of Armenians and Muslims.

After that day the Armenians carted the goods from their shops to the church and launched all kinds of oppression and bitter reproaches against the Muslims. Everyday they employed some craft or trickery. As we know, there were many government troops in the town at the time; they also insulted the residents and searched their pockets and waistbands.

In this way the population of Nakhchivan was subjected to oppression and tyranny, neither the government nor anybody else desired a complete restoration of order. Several times between then and 26 November the Muslims and the Armenians achieved peace and shook hands, owing to the efforts of the government. But these peace agreements produced only hostility and feuding. Everybody believed that a new confrontation could break out at any moment. On 26 November, the people in the bazaar suddenly closed the doors and windows of their shops in haste and ran home. When they were asked what had happened, they rubbed their hands and looked at the questioner in amazement. Various rumours were spreading among the people. News arrived from Cheshmebasar, too. Cossacks on their way there to restore peace and order had, themselves, looted the house of Haji Nasir Haji Nagi oglu. One of the sons of the family had been killed when he tried to stop them. Seeing his son in a pool of blood, the poor father fired at the Cossacks. They immediately murdered the whole family.

This news upset and disappointed the people of Nakhchivan. They understood that all the problems originated from men like Colonel Krylov and chief of police Angil; they were the founders and initiators of hostilities. On 26 November a misfortune befell the Muslims; it also revealed the cunning of the government. That night is called the night of misfortune, the night of fire and flames in Nakhchivan. It really was a night full of fire, a heartbreaking night, and very painful. At seven o'clock in the evening terrible shrieks and cries were heard. Then it became clear that they were coming from the watchmen in the bazaar. Sometimes rifle shots were heard, too. The troubled people attempted to approach the bazaar, but the Cossacks opened fire from all sides and did not allow them to approach.

The shooting continued for two hours and left the people confused and frightened. Then it stopped, silence fell. Soon the town was covered in smoke, a weak light illuminated the place.

The bazaar looked like a burning mountain, or a volcano, it was in such a state. After an hour it became obvious that the Cossacks and the Armenians, acting in concert, had stripped the Muslim shops in the bazaar completely and then set them on fire. Groans and shrieks rose high into the heavens from all quarters of the town. Within an hour the distressed people had filled the streets and squares. They were in confusion. The roar and thunder of the bazaar in flames, the cries of the people, particularly the rattle of the rifles and the loud yells of the Cossacks caused tumult in the town.

A crowd of three hundred rushed into the bazaar and saw that their property had been burnt to ashes. The Cossacks, having already won a reputation for being immoral and unjust, had burned everything and closed the roads. After two hours Angil and Krylov went to the bazaar, ordered the Cossacks to drive the people out and then they began to talk. Some minutes later they ordered the Cossacks to open fire; they killed poor Meshedi Hasan, son of Mammadgulu bey. The crowd dispersed and went home, not knowing what to do. Some Georgians, very humane, who happened to be at the railway station, came to help the Muslims (God bless them), but it was too late. The bazaar had burned to ashes by dawn.

In the morning, when the people came to the bazaar, they saw little there but the reddened earth. The shops that remained smoked for three days and nights. Approximately 85 shops and their goods, 75 store-houses and empty shops had burned out. For three days, that is, from 27 November to 30 November, there was no food to buy in the bazaar. The population suffered; in many houses people could not sleep at night because of hunger. On 29 November, at about 7 o'clock in the evening, a loud rumble was heard. The residents did not dare to go out and see what was happening. An hour later the news came in. In the second quarter of the town a Muslim house close to the Cossacks' base had been fired upon by the same Cossacks' guns and it had been looted. Half an hour later the sound of shooting echoed again; again it was the Cossacks.

On 30 November, the Muslim part of the village of Jahri was set on fire by the Cossacks and Armenians acting together. This upset the Muslims very much. On the same day Paskevich[*], the Governor General of Irevan, came to Nakhchivan; the residents assembled and asked him to do something. They also spoke about the tragedy in Jahri. In reply to their appeals the governor general said only, "Never mind, I shall investigate the case fairly," and the residents went home. The governor general feasted for two days and, when

---

[*] At that time the Governor of the Province was Secret Advisor V.F. Tizengauzen (1896-1916).

Jahri was completely in ruins, he went there. On 2 December, as the governor general was leaving, the residents told him that the Cossacks had set the second quarter of the town on fire and demanded that he take them out of the town. "Well, I have already said, mera (measures) will be taken, I shall go to Jahri, then return and take the necessary measures," so saying, he left the town.

Wasn't it the government's response which led to such a situation? The Muslims returned home, they wanted to write a complaint on behalf of all the residents and submit it to the governor. They also wanted him to take measures in connection with the tragedy in Jahri. The governor returned at 11 o'clock at night, took the train and left for Irevan, without informing the Muslims of his departure. This is the hazy veil that the bureaucratic administration draped over events for the Muslims. The proverb says: misery is the most inveterate tyrant.

I must add to the above that the Armenians suffered in the first events, but then it was the Muslims' turn.

Events in Irevan

Dealing with the events which began in Irevan in May 1905. This chapter is based on letters sent to newspapers and magazines and collected by Mir Abbas Mir Bagirzade.[*]

Disclosure of the purpose

The regrettable events which suddenly erupted in Baku did not spread everywhere, but were echoed in the Nakhchivan district of Irevan province at the beginning of May. In Nakhchivan the Muslims exceeded the Armenians in number and reputation. Nevertheless, the Armenians began fighting with the Muslims, but were finally defeated and this left a dark stain on their national history. The defeat of the Armenians in Nakhchivan enraged the Armenians of Irevan further.

Following these events, base and brutal acts by Armenians against the Muslims became increasingly frequent. People understood from the course of events that, sooner or later, troubles and riots would begin in Irevan. With such concerns the people were worried, trade began to slacken day by day and the town fell into dismay.

There were also various rumours among the Muslims, which made them very agitated. The growth in the enemy's strength, the lack of military preparation among the Muslims and other problems worried them greatly. The clouds of misfortune were clear and were advancing remorselessly above their heads. Imagine - if there were ten thousand Muslims in the town, after this terrible fright ten thousand thoughts were written across their countenances. Disappointment among the Muslims had reached a peak; there was

---

[*] Mir Abbas Mir Bagirzade - socio-political figure, later a member of the Muslim Society of Irevan Province.

a common grief and fear on their faces.

As for the Armenians, we must say that they were impatient for revenge. They were constructing strategies and tactics to draw the Muslims into conflict. Undaunted by the fact that most of the road to Nakhchivan was under Muslim control, they tried everything to render assistance to the Armenians there. And this assistance included fire-arms and ammunition. This puzzled the Muslims, we must record that the Muslims of Irevan lacked supplies, arms and ammunition. Besides, a nationalist spirit had not yet been awakened in them; it would be fair to say that it was completely absent. Everyone thought only of his own security; his heart bleeding with fear. Finally, General Alikhanov Avarski* was sent from Tiflis to extinguish the flames of terror in Nakhchivan. To suppress the conflict, His Excellency Vorontsov-Dashkov also sent Sheik-ul-Islam** Ulukhanli to the railway station; the Gazi of Irevan left with him for Nakhchivan. The Armenians heard that the government wanted peace between the two nations. Nevertheless, they were still sending people to get information from Nakhchivan, to convey information to them, helping them as they did and trying to expose the deficiencies and faults of the Muslims and to draw attention to them. The defeat of the Armenians in Nakhchivan heartened the Muslims. They thought of it as their own victory; it pleased them and they indulged in their own dreams. But the Armenians were making intensive preparations for fighting and were waiting for a cause. Then, on 23 May, an incident took place which served as a good pretext.

News of disturbances

On 23 May 1905, three educated Muslim youth were found drunk and disorderly in Garachay Gardens, in front of the police station. The Armenians took this as a pretext and beat them as

---

* Alikhanov - Avarski Maksud (1846-1907), Lieutenant General, killed by Dashnaks on 3 July 1907.

** Sheikh-ul-Islam - Muslim religious leader.

much as they could. The drunken youth unsheathed their daggers to defend themselves and rushed into the bazaar with a yell. It resonated across the whole bazaar (you know how loathsome is the noise of a drunken Muslim). Hearing the yell, the Muslims and the Armenians in the bazaar took to their rifles and began to fire at each other. Soon the disturbances spread through the whole bazaar. Some of the Muslims, unaware of the Armenians' scheming, left their shops unprotected and began to defend the shops of Armenians who had fled from fear. Some locked the Armenian shops with the owners inside to create the impression that nobody was there. In some parts both Armenians and Muslims committed crimes against each other. If the Muslims had risen against the Armenians on that day, a great misfortune would have befallen them, because all the Muslims were unarmed and unaware of the schemes developed by the Armenians. Nevertheless, the Muslims silenced the residents somehow, using existing neighbourly relations. The night passed in silence and peace.

The events of 24May 1905

On 24 May 1905, at about 9 o'clock in the morning, when the Muslims went to the bazaar to open their shops, the Armenians fired at them out of either carelessness or ignorance. Thank God it did not harm any Muslim, but several Armenians were wounded. At this point several soldiers arrived on the spot, fired into the air and silenced the Armenians. After some time movement in the town ceased, each side drew back into their own quarter and a terrible silence reigned. At about two o'clock intensive firing began again from all the Armenian quarters. Bullets rained down on the Muslims from hilltops, heights and windows. If anyone had said that burning bullets rained down on the earth, he would not have been mistaken. It continued the whole night until daybreak. They went unanswered, the Muslims kept silent. All were discouraged, the main point being that they had not made any preparations for fighting; they remained confused, because they had no experience of war. They had only about 20 rifles, some usable, some not, and a small number of cartridges. The rifles were mainly hunting rifles, left over from Noah's time, as they say, and were regarded as antiques. The government did not respond to the shooting by the Armenians and did not take any steps to stop them. The Armenians fired as much as they liked and attacked the Muslims from time to time. Nobody attempted to stop them. At about 12 o'clock they opened fire again, filling everyone with fear and terror. In reality the murder of people who had no experience of fighting was approaching.

The wails and cries of women and children confused the Muslim men and broke their spirit. Women, children, old and young, rich and poor, khan or commoner - each was thinking of his own fate, his own life.

This was a time when nobody thought of the problems of the nation, of its culture, its property or the state. The Muslims were unable to return fire. People living within the Armenian quarters were begging for help, everybody heard them, but the Muslims were powerless to rescue them from the spiral of disaster. The dust from exploding bombs and the smoking machinery of hell formed a dark cloud; against this cloud the bullets streaked like lightning, their red flames piercing the clouds and dazzling the eyes. Any officer, seeing the flame of death hovering over the heads of the Muslims, would have rushed to assist poor people crying for help. They would have saved these wretches somehow and taken them to the Muslim quarter under the protection of soldiers. But alas, it did not happen. Eleven people who had trusted the Armenians and remained in that dangerous quarter were murdered. They included four women, two children and five men. The Muslims who were rescued from the oppression and humiliation shed tears in torrents and the flood of misfortune they formed was enough to move anyone. Muslims who observed the scene felt their honour and pride had been damaged unimaginably. In such circumstances they would have preferred death, in such circumstances nationalist feelings were awoken in them, at least for a while.

With the arrival of volunteer soldiers, the Muslims of Irevan grew stronger in force and number. Many Kurds, Iranians and representatives of other nationalities took to arms and arrived in Irevan to defend their Muslim brothers. With the arrival of so many volunteers, the Muslim soldiers decided to march against the Armenians that night, despite everything. The Muslim elders and government officials began to reproach them and advised them to give up the idea and not to attack the Armenians. There were still about 30-40 Muslim households in the Armenian quarter.

On the fifth day of the riot the Muslims received soldiers from the government and, under their protection, took Muslims to the Muslim quarter. Again single shots were heard from both sides. In some places there were barricades. When Armenians saw Muslims, or vice-versa, they immediately aimed their rifles at them. In battles conducted at the barricades many Armenians were killed, the majority of them were former soldiers who had served in the Army. As for the Dashnaksutyun fighters, they had the most up-to-date weapons. Every volley they fired broke the hearts of Muslims. The Muslim fighters were mainly volunteers, many of them were unarmed, and they did not have rifles or Mausers in sufficient numbers... However, there were among the Muslim fighters good marksmen who had come from other places. The Muslims were surprised by the Armenian losses in the fighting. They fell in battle like wax dummies, they were killed with just a puff. As you know, the Armenians lacked tenacity, strength, fortitude and courage, because they were fighters who had taken part in the fighting in Baku and in the defeat in Nakhchivan; they had escaped to save their skins, they had been completely demoralized.

This was also connected to the fact that Armenian soldiers used to drink a lot of wine and vodka and other alcohol and, from time to time, fired by standing up behind the barricades, returning with the words "I shot a Muslim" and demanding a glass of cognac. Thus the Armenian's bullets missed the target and made them objects of derision among the other nationalities who looked on as spectators; even now they call those street fights the war of Irevan.

In short, the barricade war ended, peace was achieved in Nakhchivan, too, and every Armenian and Muslim was informed about it. And our government awoke from its sound sleep, scratched itself, cast a glance at the nation, telegraphed the Sheikh-ul-Islam, the Gazi of Irevan and the Archbishop and invited them to town. They arrived on 31 May.

The events of 31 May 1905

On 31 May the esteemed Armenian-Muslim guests, having restored peace and reconciliation, adorned the town with their arrival. After being met by the chiefs of the town and elders of the quarters, they were hosted by Abbasgulu khan Irevanski in his house; he considered this to be a great honour for him.

Most of the Muslims lived in another part of the town, not in the part where the house of Abbasgulu khan Irevanski was situated. During the days of conflict these two parts of the town had not communicated with each other. As the main part of the bazaar was in the Armenian quarter, shopping had stopped, people had put up street stalls in the quarters.

1 June 1905

On 1 June, the Sheikh-ul-Islam and the Archbishop walked to the boulevard, preached and gave advice to people. Then a temporary peace was achieved and the residents streamed back to the bazaar to resume their buying and selling. Several gardeners again returned to the town to resume their work. Then all of a sudden the shops and the bazaar were closed again. The town was filled with fear, all movement ceased. The town looked like a swaying ship about to sink. Some Armenian stores were looted in the Muslim quarters, in return the Armenians looted several Muslim houses. The temporary peace and reconciliation process was broken and the Armenian committees ordered their fighters to attack the Muslim villages.

The latest news

To organize riots in the province of Irevan, the Armenians appointed their commanders, and each commander left with his party members for the place assigned. The Muslim residents of Irevan were again filled with the fear of fighting. Sometimes the low sound of rifles was heard[7] from both sides. The Muslims thought of nothing but their lives. To tell the truth, there was no unanimity among the Muslims, and this hampered everyone and their common cause. The chiefs and nobility of Irevan were thinking of dividing the residents between the parties and each of them was eager to occupy a leading position. Thus there was great discord among the residents of Irevan, which prevented them from pursuing their daily work and affairs. The Sheikh-ul-Islam declaimed the following openly to the chiefs and nobility: "Dear residents! We have come to this town to reconcile these two hostile nations and to make peace, not to watch the noblemen of Irevan struggle for leadership and partisanship. Shame on them."[8]

When it was necessary to elect someone who could regularly visit the governor, or lead on national issues, each party nominated the head of his own tribe and wanted to make him chief, however unfit he was for any the post. They always presented themselves as

---

[7] Although the chief Armenian commanders, who were on the battlefield in Irevan, were defeated, they confused the Muslims in a number of ways by using their knowledge of military science. So, eager to defeat the Muslims they used the military trick of firing not fiercely, but from time to time. This is a trick which has been tested on battle-fields, that is, if the commander wants to attack on this wing, he orders the opening of sporadic fire on the other wing, to direct the enemy's attention to that wing and prevent him from making other moves.

[8] It becomes evident from the information emerging from Irevan that the nobility there is still sick with the disease of complacency inherent to their ancestors. When the Armenians dream of annihilating someone, they display generosity. Shame on these creatures who sustain the errors committed by their ancestors and preserve them for so long!

being skilful and they claimed leadership; it was nothing but hot air.[9]

Concerns about the defence and protection of the motherland and nation on the one hand and, on the other, the deception of the people by the nobility, who also mocked them and sowed the seeds of hostility, filled sober-minded intellectuals with disgust. In those days news came to Irevan that the Armenians had besieged the Muslims and were slaughtering them in the province.

As soon as the news reached the town, an atmosphere of funereal hopelessness engulfed the Muslim residents. They were face to face with an enemy who had surrounded them. The town itself was in the grip of strong Armenian villages, therefore, the people felt isolated and terrorized. At first, people came to Irevan and left it freely from the south, but after the riots communications were broken. The poor Muslim villages were thinking of their own fates. So everybody lived in a state of conflict. Well, it is true that a handful of Muslim villages, illiterate and without any experience of battle, was surrounded by Armenian villages which had detachments experienced in waging war and which were literate and well-informed. The Muslim residents of these villages had no support and their grave situation evoked pity. The Armenians fired from time to time in the town and threatened the Muslims and their property. The Muslims had already consigned their fates to the mercy of God, and were sure that their end was near. Their faces carried the pallor of death, they thought that it was a misfortune sent by God and, therefore, prayed and promised to give alms.[10] Those villagers who had material-financial prospects were ready to move as soon as possible. The villains thought only of themselves and their proper-

---

[9] My dear reporter! Don't grieve too much that everybody in Irevan tries to promote the head of his tribe to the position of chief of the nation. Because if you look anywhere in the Muslim world you will see men with similar disreputable intentions. It means that Muslims lack the science of humanity. Such qualities inherent in us explain a number of misadventures in the 19th century. Don't take it to heart. Our small town Ordubad has also been infected by this disease.

[10] Of course we think we will survive adversity, but we know that hope without action will not produce results.

ty and considered themselves to be superior to their motherland. "Let us save our harems and children from the spiral of death. The enemy can take the needy." Thinking this way, the villains were shameless in bearing the title of Muslim and of human being.

While the chiefs in Irevan were plotting their intrigues, blood flowed in the country; the heads of innocent people swam in pools of blood and they were tossed from pillar to post.

While the Holy Koran was being burnt in Irevan, the people who were thought to be its advocates, who were considered to be devoted to the principles of the Holy Book, were engaged in the business of party-building. When the pulpits of the mosques were set on fire, believers who went to the mosques day and night and prayed to God and did nothing else, could do nothing but put their hands to their hearts and pat. In a word, the province of Irevan was like a fiery mountain, a volcano burning and suffocating the noble Muslims.

In the east of Irevan there is a village called Girkhbulag, three-quarters of its population are Armenians, one-quarter are poor and humble Muslims. On the first day of June riots and troubles broke out, the tragedy of Gozechik took place. This small village consists of 20 households. The attack was launched by the residents of Tirjabat, an Armenian village. I shall now narrate everything in detail.

The doleful tragedy of Gozechik

On 31 May 1905, a little before evening, Armenians surrounded the village of Gozechik and subjected it to a hail of fire. Being completely unarmed, the villagers took their families to find refuge in the village of Mankus, not far from Gozechik. The Armenians continued the pursuit and wanted to attack Mankus, too. The headman of the village, Hummet bey Huseynzade, had moved to the town, there was an elderly man in the village, aged fifty, ruling the village in his place.

This elderly man, by name Novruz Kazimoglu, seeing the Muslims running, climbed to a low hilltop and said:

"People, where are you running? Young men, where are you running? Do you want to humiliate us, bring us, the Muslims of the Caucasus, into disgrace before other nations?! Will the Armenians let you live?! No, no, they will not. By running, you will encourage them more, they will abuse us and our families in ways never seen before in any century.

Are they not the same Armenians who were ready to leave the province of Girkhbulag when I shook my finger at them?! Now what has happened that you have joined poor, helpless women and flee like a flock of sheep?! If you wish, run and save your hides, go on. I shall stand alone against the battalion of Armenians and will not surrender to them alive. Muslims! Every man, every nation must leave this world with the dignity befitting his person and name.

According to the law of Prophet Muhammad it is wrong and unacceptable to flee from the enemy to save your life when you fight for the nation of Islam, for principles approved by God.

You know that the bones of our ancestors resting in this cemetery will be wrenched from their graves, taken to the Armenian villages and burnt. And in place of our cemetery they will build their Armenia here. I will not be held responsible for this in the next world; I shall try to defend the village." - With these words he finished.

The people did not listen to the words of this brave patriot and preferred to leave the village.

Novruz Kazimoglu remained in the village and became a target for the Armenians. His relatives came to rescue him from the siege, but it was too late, because of the large number of enemies they could not get through. Novruz killed one of the Armenians who tried to break down the door. He fired at the enemy with his double-barrelled shotgun. The rest retreated.

This story was related by an Armenian who was an eye-witness. A little later the Armenians attacked again. Novruz killed one more and the others were obliged to turn back. Novruz had run out of cartridges; while he was trying to fill a cartridge with birdshot, the Armenians broke into the room, set the house on fire and captured him. Then they set the mosque and the rest of the village houses on fire, also the books of the Holy Koran in the mosque. With his hands tied, they took him to the Armenian village of Tirjabat. They tortured him and cut off his head. His head was cut off by Ayrapet, the clergyman of the village church, because one of the Armenians shot by Novruz was his son. "Novruz's head is worth the heads of 1500 Muslim commanders." The head was sent first to Alexandropol, then to Baku.

The events of 2 June

On 2 June, the village of Mankus, where the Muslims had found refuge, was attacked by the Armenians. This time the armed Armenians numbered over 10,000. They fired at the village from at least 5,000 rifles. The Muslims had few arms, they took their families and retreated one by one whenever they had a chance. Then the Armenians made the final attack, the village was empty, except for an old, disabled man of eighty. It was said that he was stabbed with a spit usually used for baking bread in the oven. During the battle for Gozechik, when the Muslims were calling for help, a man by the name of Jahanbakhshbey, with two Kurdish horsemen from the village of Galadibi, some 15 farsakh[11] from there, happened to be in Mankus. The three of them occupied a position on the hilltop to the north-east of the village and fired at the Armenian detachments that were pursuing the women and children from Mankus. They killed two Armenians. Thus, the women and children found refuge in the village of Tezekend[12], about 15 farsakh away. The refugees from 12 Muslim villages found shelter there.

3 June 1905

On 3 June the Armenians attacked the village of Gulluje, which was surrounded by Armenian villages. It had 150 households.

---

[11] Farsakh - unit of measure equal to six kilometers

[12] A solitary Muslim village of 20 households in the north-east of Gart, an Armenian sanctuary.

The outbreak of fighting

On 3 June, at dawn, about 10,000 volunteer Armenian soldiers from the Armenian village of Bashkeni and from another 14 Armenian villages to the north of Gulluje, each of them of about 400 households, fired intensively at Gulluje. The Armenians' goal was to subjugate the Muslims, to enslave them, to make them their vassals, or to exterminate all of them and build the independent state for which they yearned so much. To this end the Armenians of the province took to arms and moved against the Muslims. Being unarmed, the residents of Gulluje left the village, which was soon occupied by the Armenians. When the villagers left, there remained rich residents by the names of Meshedi Ganbar, Mahmud, Haji Huseyn and others, 15 men in all, to defend their property. They killed eight Armenians. Finally Mahmud was killed. An old, helpless woman, who did not have anybody to take care of her, was also murdered, by eight bullets. The rest retreated and found refuge in the nearby Muslim villages of Tutya, Damagirmez and Kamal. In this hasty retreat, a man by the name of Mir Suleyman Seyid Mustafa oglu was the last to leave the village. The Armenians shot his horse; in return he killed an Armenian and escaped.

The events of 4 June

On 4 June, the village of Kamal, with its 150 households, remained isolated by the Armenian siege. Seeing the danger, its residents, including women and children, moved to the village of Damagirmez, located on the plain to the south. Then the residents of this village also joined them and took refuge in the aforementioned village of Tezekend, which was about 20 versts from there.

They remained in Tezekend for 18 days, suffering from hunger and thirst. Then peace was achieved again in Irevan, troops were sent to all the abandoned villages, a detachment of soldiers arrived at the village of Gulluje. Only then did the Muslims return home.

Echmiadzin. The Events in Uchkilse

(Summary of letters)

After the riots in Irevan and surrounding villages, it became clear that the Muslims were not trained in the art of war. Besides, they did not have the arms and ammunition to help the villages subjected to Armenian aggression. Thus the Armenians were encouraged and attacked the province of Girkhbulag and defeated the Muslims.

Further, they murdered and looted the Muslims of Uchkilse,* exploiting the village's unfavourable geographical location, and subjected the Muslims to unimaginable tortures and humiliations.

The geographical location of Echmiadzin

Echmiadzin is located on a vast area between the rivers Khanavenk and Anpur and is famous for its natural scenery and fruit orchards. To the west are the Alayiz Mountains, the Abaran region and the provinces of Alexandropol, Panbak and Shoragol. In its west is the water basin of the Anapur, in the east - the River Khanavenk and the province of Irevan. In its south is the ancient Armenian sanctuary and centre of Uchkilse*.

The Armenian riots of 1905 against the Muslims and military mobilization

On 3 June, the Armenians of Shoragel, Panbak and Alexandropol from the Abaran region assembled and attacked the Muslim village of Ushu. On that day fortifications were built all around the Armenian village of Ilanchalan and the Muslim village

---

*Literally, "Three churches".

of Ushu, and the battle began at 9 o'clock in the morning. After a violent struggle, which continued for eight hours, the Armenians could not hold out against the Muslims: they suffered serious losses and were obliged to retreat in haste. Those who escaped threw themselves desperately into the River Khanavenk, many of them drowning there, the rest crossed to the other bank and saved themselves. The Muslim youth did not miss a single target, the bullets pierced the breasts of the Armenians and many of them lay dead on the battle-field. On 4 June the Armenians decided to postpone the fighting, they were discouraged and not yet ready to continue the battle. "We can not defeat the Muslims with such a small force," they said and again began to mobilize soldiers from the nearby provinces and villages. Members of various Armenian parties, mounted and on foot, arrived and joined the Armenian detachments, right before the Muslims' eyes. The roads to the Muslim village were closed by the Armenians on all four sides, no one came to help them. Even before the start of fighting the Armenians had blockaded the village, it was impossible to enter from any direction. The Armenians attacked the village from the north, the other three sides being blockaded.

5 June

On 5 June, the Armenians attacked the village. After several attempts sustained losses, they were repulsed and withdrew to their fortifications. The Muslims had two men killed and one wounded. The situation being critical, the Armenians halted the battle on the sixth and seventh of June and went out again to mobilize soldiers and adjust their preparations for battle. Their trenches were guarded by soldiers on all sides.

The events of 8 June

On this day the Muslims were attacked from all sides. The Armenians used rifles, and thus did not incur significant losses. For this reason, the Muslims remained in their trenches and were unable to launch sudden attacks against the enemy, and they suffered losses. Further, the Muslims did not have sufficient ammunition or other equipment necessary for battle. They gradually abandoned the fortification and withdrew back to the village. They realised that it was useless to continue the battle, nevertheless they rushed onto the attack, determined not to surrender the village to the enemy while they were alive. They assembled the women and children in the mosque and continued the fight.

Battle inside the village

Two hours before evening, soldiers of the Armenian parties attacked the village from all sides. An old priest carrying a military flag led the Armenians into battle. They were singing a song. In his other hand the priest had a cross and he was encouraging the soldiers to fight.

In this battle the only actions to damage the Armenians' reputation were the initial killings of suckling babies and old women. Recognising the inevitability of the Armenian attack, a Muslim by the name of Pasha Budag oglu went to the mosque and led the women and children away into the high mountains; crossing many incredibly difficult paths and roads, they found shelter with the Kurdish tribes in Surmeli. Less than an hour before dusk, battles began inside the village. In the dim of the evening in fighting with daggers, the Muslims lost two disabled and two elderly men. The Muslims fought with daggers, the Armenians with rifles. Nevertheless, 180 Armenians were killed and approximately the same number were wounded. The Armenians outnumbered the Muslims 15 to 1 and so the Muslims decided to leave the village. The Armenians set it on fire. Everything holy, even the books of the Holy Koran and other items, were burnt. The damage done to the Muslims amounted to about two hundred thousand manats. Then the Armenians attacked the Muslim village of Tekya. The following villages were destroyed in this battle: Persi, Nazveran, Kichikkend, Kotuklu, Goshabulag, Irgu on the bank of the River Anapur and Enkirsek - seven large well-populated villages.

The battle of Tekya on 9 June 1905

On 9 June, at about 12 o'clock, the Armenians attacked the Muslim village of Tekya. The residents of the village were completely unarmed and so they could not stand against the Armenians with their modern rifles. They took their families and withdrew to the highlands. The enemy set on fire the house of Akhund Muhammad Ali Mirza Huseyn and burned his two hundred books, his Holy Koran and other holy books. His library and books belonging to the Office of Gazi were destroyed. When a servant looked down on the village from the hilltop, he saw how the Armenians bayonetted the Holy Korans and burned them. Thinking that Muslims were hiding in the mosque, the Armenians fired at it so much that its walls looked like honeycomb. Then they burned the pulpit and other holy articles in the mosque. On 10 June, nine large Muslim villages were destroyed; the government took no action.[13]

---

[13] Letters came to me from all corners of the country. The government displayed indifference and did nothing, as ever. I hope that the two nations understand well the significance.

Events in Jabrail and Karyagin

On 13 June 1905, riots began in Jabrail and Karyagin in Ganja province.

Through the newspaper *Irshad*, I asked readers to inform me about the events which were taking place there. Then I received a journal from Mirza Jamal Yusifzade and letters from the province with a description of events. After editing, I published them.

My conclusions

The letters I received tell of the Armenians' desire: they demand independence or, at least, autonomy. There are many controversial opinions concerning the events in Jabrail, but actual facts will put an end to readers' doubts.

As for my own view, I think that the Armenians' efforts are in vain, a waste of time, I can not say anything else about this. The Armenians tested their forces in many ways and inflicted injuries on the Muslims, nevertheless they were defeated. We must bear in mind that the Muslims did not have military forces, firearms or a regular army with battle experience. In addition, government officials helped the Armenians in some ways. If we remember that they had been preparing to fight for twenty years, then we understand their villainy. Some people say that the Armenians are against Russia, or Turkey; this is childish, I think.

Disclosure of the purpose

On 13 June 1905, two armed soldiers of the Armenian Dashnaksutyun Party came to the village of Gajar and said the following to Ahmad Karbalayi Gasim oglu, a resident of the village:

"The two of us, are members of the Dashnaksutyun Party. We

have been charged by men in authority to convey to you, the Muslim people, the following words written here. The authorities of the Dashnaksutyun Party invite you to the well-known Agoglan monastery on 16 June.[14] The villages noted below have already been informed about this. If you come there at the appointed time, you will hear words important for you. The other villages are: Divanali, Yaglivend, Dilagarda and Veisalli."

On 16 June, the majority of the inhabitants of these villages went to the monastery to a meeting held there.

Description of the monastery

A meeting was held in the Agoglan monastery of the Armenian and Muslim populations. It took place in the monastery yard. Tables and chairs were set out. In the centre there were three decorated armchairs, intended for the Armenian leaders.

Soon the said authoritative persons entered the meeting and took their seats in the armchairs. Two minutes later, that is, just after the official introduction, an Armenian by the name of Bakhshi rose from his seat and appealed to the audience. The Armenians did not want him to continue his speech, nevertheless he said the following: "Men, these three reliable guests have come to your province, to your village as guests. My name is Bakhshi, and I am from the village of Chartaz. My real name is Ashot. I perform the service of secretary and interpreter to these three distinguished persons. The man in the armchair is a highly esteemed person"...The Armenians shouted and hushed him. Then the man sitting in the armchair on the right rose from his seat proudly and majestically, and made the following speech:

The text of the first speech

"Gentlemen, we, the Armenians, the Muslims, all the Caucasians, need to assemble and discuss all issues and make the

---

[14] This monastery is located between the Muslim village of Gajar and the Armenian village of Changchi

people understand everything. Because we, particularly the Muslims, are completely unaware of culture and science, are deprived of the light of culture and science. Of course, if one possesses the light of culture and science, then one understands the real meaning of the word light. Therefore, we can not achieve anything without discussing our common problems. I address my words exclusively to the Armenians and the Muslims. You all know that we, the Caucasians, now live under the yoke and oppression of the Russians, they do with us whatever they wish and whatever they can. They have practised tyranny and mercilessness against us so often. They have trampled on our human rights and our right to independence, they have deprived us of our actual and individual rights!

We, the Armenian nation, have for a long time been claiming our national rights and independence, that is, independent governance. But Russia, which is our enemy, is like a huge elephant. We and you, more exactly, the non-Russian peoples, have always been weak and humble, helpless, have always been afraid of the despotism of the government, have lived in hunger and poverty, in fear of that huge elephant. But thank God, the Japanese, who are as small as flies, more helpless than we, have delivered such a heavy blow to that elephant, that it has brought us closer to our goal.* Those flies have pursued the despot elephant so much and tired him so much that, finally, he has fallen into a ditch, into a deep channel, on his back. Now, brothers, let us unite and destroy the flesh of that elephant piece by piece.

Perhaps by destroying the flesh and blood of that elephant, the light of justice may fall on the fates of nations who have been living in ignorance and oppression, and they may become safe. Well, brothers, it is high time for us to unite." In this way he finished his speech. Then the man on the left rose solemnly and delivered the following:

---

* The Russian-Japanese war of 1904-1905 is meant here; it ended with the defeat of Tsarist Russia.

The text of the second speech

"Gentlemen! We, the Armenian nation, have been dreaming for a long time of having a big pot to cook a meal of justice, including equality, and sharing this meal with you and several other nations. Now that pot is ready and we need a tripod to stand the pot on. One of its legs is the Armenians, the second is the Georgians, we want you, the Muslims, to be the third leg. Of course, it is necessary for our Muslim brothers to listen to us and be the third leg of that tripod. In this matter we rely on the Muslims." He also finished his speech.[15] Then the third man, who seemed very reserved, rose to his feet majestically, delivered a speech and directed several questions to the audience.

The text of the third speech

You, our kind neighbours, noble Muslims! We have lived with you side by side for many years. Have you not heard that some time ago the government captured our arms and ammunition in Uchkilse-Echmiadzin?" The Muslims answered: "Yes, we have! " "Haven't you heard about the firearms captured in Shusha, from the cemetery?" The Muslims again responded: "Yes, we have!" Then it is clear that we have made good preparations for war and obtained arms and ammunition; there will be enough, not only for us, but for you, too. If you have courage and diligence, we have enough arms and money for you. Together with you we shall use the arms that we obtained with so much difficulty. Otherwise, those arms will be used against you and bring misfortune to you. Of course, if you do not help us in this matter, the lightning of misfortune will strike you and turn your motherland into ruins. Your houses will become graveyards, your children will be buried in the dismal corners of

---

[15] When we first spoke about the events in Shusha, we mentioned the desire of the Armenians for autonomy; this was our understanding, and that of our friendly Georgian brothers. Thus, we do not think there is a need to repeat it here.

those graveyards". With these words he took his seat. The Muslims protested and the meeting was over.[16]

Muslim protests against the Armenians' speeches

When the Armenian nationalists had finished their speeches, they also issued oral threats against the Muslims. The Muslims did not like these views and, in protest against them, the following residents of the village of Gajar rose to their feet. Gasimzade Molla Abdurrahim and then Tapdiq Talibkhanov said this:

"You, the Armenians, do not know us, the Muslims, well! We have never been frightened by such threats. Of course, our Muslim nation is not your army! And we do not need your arms and provisions. If we desire to fight, then we shall make our own preparations. Are we fool enough, or asleep, to take your arms and rise against our brothers?! Our nation and villages say the contrary," he finished his speech. All the Muslims rose and in said in chorus: "We are not your partners in such things," they moved to leave the monastery.

One of the three Armenian chiefs rose from his seat and said: "Muslims, stop a minute, stop a minute! I have one more thing to say. Let me finish, then go." The Muslims stopped. The Armenian continued: "Besides us, the three Armenian chiefs, there are also party functionaries who want you to hear these words. If the Muslims present at this meeting do not accept our proposal, they will be subject to punishment by Dashnaksutyun troops. "Never mind, never mind," said the Muslims and the meeting ended.

---

[16] I took the words from an esteemed reporter of the truth and published the texts of the speeches without any changes, my present work being far removed from any nationalism or personal bias, I shook the texts of letters through the sieve of criticism and published them. In answer to the threats of the last speaker a Muslim said: "Dear sir, the Muslims of Jabrail are not made of honey wax. We also have hands and eyes. But if you want to know our opinion, we are for peace for all."

News of the disturbances

Following this meeting the lightning of misfortune mentioned by the Armenian nationalists crackled across Shusha. It is known that when the Armenians delivered a blow against the Muslims, they got two in reply. So the Armenians missed an opportunity here. The disturbances spread like an infection and destroyed homes. They finally penetrated the district of Jabrail. And Divanali, a rich village and popular with its 25 households, became a target for Armenian attacks. When the Armenians attacked the village, the Muslims did not resist strongly, they took their families and property and left the village. It was soon looted and set on fire. The Armenians pulled down the houses and transported the precious stones and wood to the Armenian village of Sust. Since then the residents of Divanali have been homeless and live in poverty like beggars. The barbarians cut down all the fruit trees in the village's gardens and carted them away. In this way they left no shelter for the Muslims to dwell in and did everything to turn the village into ruins.

About the tragedies in the village of Veisalli

After the destruction of Divanali, the Armenians supplied the residents of the Armenian village of Chartaz[17] with arms and, together with the inhabitants of other Armenian villages, they attacked the Muslim village of Veisalli.

The Armenians surrounded the village and fired at it from all sides. The Muslims were few in number, nevertheless, they put up strong resistance to the enemy, who soon lost 15 persons killed. One Muslim was murdered, the rest were obliged to abandon the village.

Their Armenian neighbours destroyed the village, looted it and set it on fire. A Muslim who watched the scene related that an Armenian neighbour who had frequently been the guest of a

---

[17] Chartaz is a rich Armenian village of 950 houses.

Muslim's family and had eaten and drunk in his house, was the most active. He was the first to set his host's house on fire. The residents of the village suffered great damage.

*The events in the village of Gajar**

After the painful events of Veisalli, the Dashnaks launched an attack on the village of Gajar, which had 150 households. The events in Gajar were completely different. Three hours before daybreak, officers commanded by General Aslan bey Melikshahnazarov[18] of the Dashnaksutyun party supplied the residents of Armenian villages with arms and together they attacked Gajar.

The Armenian forces taking part in the attack on the village of Gajar

Ashot with his soldiers from the village of Chartaz, Beyler bey from the village of Chikhaduz, Sanjan bey from the village of Mavag with members of his party, an Armenian commander named Sago with the Zengezur regiments assembled at a place called Vabayjan, two versts west of Gajar. This spot served as headquarters. They made all the preparations for the attack and formed a military council to conduct it. The commanders received instructions from the council.

Battle preparations, or the military plan

Melikshahnazarov's soldiers were ordered to attack Gajar from Mount Khazaz in the west and Ishkhanov's soldiers - from Mount Ojagli in the south. The Armenian commander Marshal Sago was ordered to attack from the west by linking the western parts of the two mountains. The above-named commanders occupied their positions at night and stood ready for the signal from Commander Sago.

---

* see map on page 87.

[18] Aslan bey's first name was Sograt, he was from the Chanakchi beys.

Outbreak of hostilities

An hour and half before dawn Commander Sago signalled the beginning of the attack with a musical march. They set up continuous fire from their repeater rifles at Gajar. The residents, who were fast asleep, awoke in fear and saw the village in a commotion. Babies sucking at their mothers' breasts were frightened, broke off and began to cry. The wailing of women, groaning of the children, the yelling and noises of various animals merged and it seemed like the Day of Judgment. Above it all sounded the ruthless crack of the Armenian rifles.

Oil lamps were extinguished out of fear, but in those houses where the lamps had gone out at night, they were now lit. Nobody understood yet what was happening in the village of about one thousand people. Each had his own thoughts, fear rose in their hearts. The people were in confusion, one was running to his neighbour, another was rousing his landlord, others were frozen with fear and remained as still as an ornament on the wall. On the other hand, the Muslim volunteers, men of valour and courage, did not lose their heads, they began to dig trenches around the village and each of them stood face to face with a detachment of Armenian soldiers. The women and children could not stay at home and they joined the men in the trenches. After six hours of fierce battle, 55 houses not far from the fortifications, were set on fire and looted. Then the Armenians decided to take the Muslim women captive and they launched an all-out assault against the Muslim trenches. May God help the Muslim fighters, bravo! Praise be to their valour and courage. The Armenians could not stand against them, they suffered great losses and retreated to their previous positions. The Muslims displayed resolution, left their trenches and attacked the enemy. Some Muslim villages heard the news, mounted their horses and, armed with guns, marched to the battlefield in Gajar. The first to arrive was Hasanali bey Askerkhanov, a resident of the village of Yaglivend, with twenty armed horsemen. As soon as they reached Mount Khazaz, they fired at the Melikshahnazarov detachment. Hasanli bey approached the trenches fearlessly and forced the Armenians to leave their positions, and then he occupied the top of Mount Khazaz. As soon as he had accomplished this he instructed his horsemen and continued the attack. Disregarding the siege, the Muslims broke it, and with daggers in their hands they jumped into man-to-man combat.

Ashot, the Armenian officer mentioned above, was killed, together with his soldiers in the trench. The Muslims were so enraged that their eyes were blood-red, they fought fiercely. Although they had already gained superiority over the enemy, the Muslim volunteers streamed in from all sides to help. Their number grew by the hour. The Armenians were also trying to begin an all-out attack to suppress the Muslims. The Armenian cavalry commanded by Ishkhanov rained down bullets from the top of Mount Ojagli.

When the number of Muslims was sufficient, they left the trenches and jumped into hand-to-hand battle, tangling everywhere with the Armenians.

The hand-to-hand fighting continued for four hours. They used daggers and bayonets. The Armenians were demoralized and discouraged. They lost courage and gradually began to retreat. The young Muslim volunteers blocked their ways back, the Armenians suffered great losses. The Muslim cavalry began to pursue the retreating Armenians. The latter left a rear guard, but the battle continued and the Muslims pursued the enemy for ten versts. On their way back they destroyed and looted the Armenian village of Afshar and took three captives. The retreating Armenian commanders supplied their soldiers with the necessary equipment and, with three thousand fighters, made a second attempt to attack the village of Gajar. They issued the following orders to their own soldiers:

"First, kill the whole male population of Gajar and capture all the female residents and distribute them among the Armenians.

Second, fight to the death of the last Armenian soldier".

Thank God the Armenians could not achieve their goal and were defeated. During the battle of Gajar the Muslims suffered a great loss of property, but only 12 men were killed. On the field of battle, 150 Armenians were killed and about 200 were wounded, but they returned to the locations where they served. According to some Armenians, they lost nearly 253 men.

The final events in the districts of Jabrail and Karyagin

After the dreadful tragedy in Baku, real respect emerged between the Armenians and Muslims in Karyagin. There was nothing to instigate conflict or war between them. Nevertheless, this love was superficial and deceptive, and was aimed at weakening the nationalist feelings and spirit of the Muslims, at giving them a false sense of security. There are many facts supporting this, and there is no need for further proof. So, after the first tragic events in Shusha, a resident of the town, Mursal Haji Gulu oglu, hosted a feast in Garabulag bazaar, in Karyagin, and invited many local government officials, noblemen and merchants, including Isfendiyar bey Vezirov and Agabey Ishkhanov.

Agabey Ishkanov was an Armenian cavalry officer. On his way he met Isfendiyar bey. The latter asked him: "You have promised Mursal to go to the dinner party, where are you going now?" "I shall come in time", was the reply. In the evening when Isfendiyar bey was on his way to the dinner party, he entered a pharmacy owned by an Armenian named Grisha, the latter asked him the following questions:

"Isfendiyar bey, why did you not ask the police chief's secretary, Israil Teroganesov, where Agabey Ishkhanov was going?" He replied:

"I saw him myself on my way here." Hearing this reply Grisha said:

"I beg you to go and ask him once more."

Isfendiyar bey:

"Well, tell me, why should I ask Israil?"

Grisha repeated:

"Ask Israil about it."

After such a question, Isfendiyar bey said to himself:

"Oh, my ignorant head, perhaps Agabey has gone off again to do something wrong, he is an Armenian commander," then he set off impatiently to find Israil, to find out what the matter was:

"Israil, where has Agabey gone?"

"Agabey has fallen from his horse and broken some bones. He has been taken to the village of Chiraguz." Isfendiyar bey, full of doubt and deep in thought, left for Mursal's dinner party.

News of the riots

Several days after the dinner party, the Armenians trading in the bazaar collected their goods in haste and left. This seemed very unnatural to everybody. When they were asked the reason for such haste, they did not reply, but continued to flee. Much later it became evident that fighting had broken out in Shusha. To learn the truth, the Muslims sent telegrams to Shusha, but they received this reply: "There is nothing of the kind." After a lapse of several days the Armenians again returned to the bazaar and began trading as usual. They had fled because of the outbreak of fighting; they had carried away the most expensive goods and emptied the shops.

Then it became clear that just three Armenians had remained in the bazaar.

The Muslims grew suspicious, they appealed to the post-office and learned that intensive battles were going on in Shusha. When they heard the news, Muslims from everywhere gathered in the village of Shikhli for a conference. The people at the assembly, including residents of Shusha, decided to go to Shusha, they mounted their horses and set off. Some time later, armed residents of Jabrail and Karyagin joined them and moved forward along the Agdam road. 300 cavalry from Jabrail followed the Molla Nesreddin road and assembled in the village of Sheikhmali, which is in a neighbourhood of the Jabrail-Karyagin district. They spent the night in the village with sentries stationed. They sent out scouts in all directions. They learned that the information about Agabey Ishkanov's fall from his horse had been a lie. He had collected a large number of soldiers and conducted military training on a vast plain called Nur Muhammad's *Deyirman*[*].

When the Muslims heard the news they said: "It would be madness to leave the Armenians here and go to Shusha." They sent several men in disguise to learn all about Agabey's military forces.

Letters from the fighting

The Muslims tried to learn more about the enemy forces, but could not get much information. Nevertheless, the scouts found out that Agabey had about 1,000 cavalry and infantry under his command.

The Muslims had 500 cavalry and 300 infantry volunteers. With this force they decided to attack Agabey's detachment. First the snipers, that is, the good shots, moved forward. As soon as they were within range, they fired at the enemy's position. Then the Muslim infantry broke the enemy's defences and fired at its right wing. On the left wing more Muslim infantry rushed the enemy and threatened it with destruction.

The Armenians had not divided their troops into detachments, they were commanded by one person and began the battle in a single formation. The Muslim snipers, organized from the infantry, pinned down the enemy forces. The cavalry behind them fired at the Armenian cavalry and separated them from the infantry. The battle began at dawn and continued until the afternoon. Four hours before dusk the Armenians could not repel the Muslim attacks and were obliged to flee. When the Muslim commanders saw the Armenians in retreat, they withdrew the infantry and ordered the cavalry to pursue the enemy. The Armenians ran in disorder and panic, not even providing the retreating soldiers with a rear guard, thus they suffered great losses. They rushed into an Armenian village called Dudukchu. The Muslim infantry snipers sealed the exits from the village and the most significant positions around it. Then

---

[*] *Deyirman* - Mill

the Muslim cavalry attacked. The Armenians lost ten men, left the village and tried to flee. It was close to dusk, the battlefield was very uneven, rocky and with many paths, and so the Muslims did not pursue the enemy, but destroyed and looted the village. They captured Ishkhanov with his horse and also took several horses as trophies. As in previous cases, the Armenians hid their losses. The Muslims saw many wounded Armenian soldiers moaning and breathing their last. During a battle which had started at dawn and continued until evening, the Muslims did not suffer any losses and returned to their detachments giving thanks to God and Prophet Muhammad.

The battle of Chemenli

At sunrise, the watchmen announced that the Armenians had attacked the village of Chemenli. Having left a security detachment at the site of the previous day's battle, the Muslims marched off to Chemenli in military order. At the same time, an Armenian detachment marched there from the direction of the Armenian village of Akhullu. Having assessed the situation, the Muslims divided into three detachments and confronted the Armenians from three directions. In the battle, the Muslim infantry courageously barred the Armenians' retreat and began to apply pressure. The Armenians were in a difficult situation, after a fierce battle and tried to retreat to Akhullu, however, one verst from the main battleground, they were met by a detachment of Muslim cavalrymen who were waiting in ambush and who launched a shattering attack on the enemy. Having surrounded Akhullu on all sides, they dislodged the Armenians and put them to flight.

In that battle the enemy suffered great losses; the exact number was impossible to determine because of the falling darkness. Only Jabrail Jafargulu oghlu of the Muslims died, from wounds he had received. Leaving a military guard in the village, the Muslims returned to rejoin their force.

The battle of Agbulag

The next day, intelligence said that at sunrise the Armenians were again gathered around the Armenian village of Agbulag and were preparing for a new assault on Chemenli. Having received this information the Muslims, fully equipped and in military order, moved to protect Chemenli. The battle in Agbulag can be considered the most difficult one in that war. The Armenians started the battle cautiously, while the Muslims went onto the offensive along the entire front. The bloody battle continued until evening. The Armenian detachments were completely routed, retreated to Agbulag and continued shooting from cover behind the houses. The Muslims, having surrounding the village, subjected it to continuous firing, dislodged the Armenians from Agbulag, ransacked and devastated the village. As usual, the Armenians hid the true scale of their losses. Not even one Muslim died in that battle and the whole force, thank Allah, returned to their placement. They did not finish off the wounded Armenians, considering them already dead.

The battle of Arish

The day after the battle of Agbulag, the Armenians gathered in the Armenian village of Khirmanjig, which had 250 households, and collected soldiers from all the nearby Armenian villages. Their forces now numbered about 2500. They supplied the soldiers with arms and ammunition. This time they were longing to defeat the Muslims and restore lost glory.

The village of Khirmanjig was surrounded by mountains; access to the village was not easy because of its impassable roads and pathways. At least 10,000 fighters and supplies were needed to occupy and keep the village under siege for a month or two.

Assembling in the village of Khirmanjig, the Armenians intended to attack the Muslim village of Arish and destroy it or, in the event of defeat, to rush back to Khirmanjig and save themselves.

It was impossible to enter the village from any side, it was mountainous territory and there was only one narrow road, with room for barely a single horseman. There were also pathways impassable by even one rider. Muslim scouts collected information on the forces, strength and mood of the Armenians and delivered it to their commander.

The Muslims then restored their forces, took up battle positions, summoned forces from their head quarters in the village of Sheikhmali and from other places, and assembled them in the village of Arish to begin battle in the following manner in advance of the Armenians.

Letters from the war, or news from the battlefield

The Muslim commanders were well aware of the enemy forces. They made speeches to their soldiers, instilling devotion and courage. The soldiers became excited, their blood on the boil. They declared to their commanders that they were the sons of heroic soldiers. At this very moment the Muslim guards informed the commanders that the Armenians had begun to move from the village of Khirmanjig an hour before dawn. The Commander-in-Chief gave instructions to the detachment commanders and sent them to occupy positions in the trenches around the village. They were informed about every movement of the Armenians. When the soldiers were ready to fight, the Commander-in-Chief mounted his horse and addressed the fighters thus:

"My sons! In any event I regret that relations between the Muslims and the Armenians have been aggravated and reached such a peak. Nevertheless, regret will do no good, either to the Muslims, or the Armenians. Because we are compelled to stand face to face with them and fight. In this hour nothing else is of any use to us. Only rifles and daggers will help us! Yes, rifles and daggers! In times of peace it is necessary to make peace, in times of war - to wage war. Do you know how many Muslim villages have been destroyed by the Armenians? Do you know how many of our daughters, sisters and wives have been taken captive by them?

What humiliations and tortures have they been subjected to? But do not worry! However bitter this captivity, this humiliation, do not worry! You also know that on the battlefield at Karbala, Huseyn Ibn Ali (Hail to him) stood with a handful of his closest men against criminal detachments numbered in the hundreds of thousands and led by Yazid (God damn him).

He was the embodiment of freedom and courage. His bravery on the field of battle in Karbala did not blind the eyes to truth. He did not ask for mercy from Yazid, the son of an unknown father. Yes, he did not obey Yazid, and so his children and men became captives. But we have one difference from His Excellency. That difference is that his sisters, wives, daughters were related to Ali ibn Abu Talib, therefore, no one in the army of Yazid would dare to insult or humiliate them. But you must know, brothers, what will happen if your wives are captured by the Armenians?!"

(There were loud cries among the soldiers). He continued his speech:

"In our Muslim law, to ensure one's defence is an important matter. Therefore you must defeat the fear and cowardice in your hearts. Fear and cowardice are culpable and unacceptable qualities, incompatible with the struggle for motherland and nation. Fear contradicts Islam and humanity. If your eyes fear the dagger of the enemy, they will meet death, your wealth and property will be looted, our wives and sisters will be captured. It is the same whether you die in your bed, or in the wilderness, if you drown in the ocean, or if you die under the enemy's dagger. One thing is clear: you die only once. Our triumph in this war, our death in pools of blood will remain in the pages of history and serve the independence of the nation and the sons of the motherland.

The blood of courage we shed on the rocks of Khirmanjig will never be wiped away. Our children will see that we martyred ourselves to preserve the name of Islam. Of course, if you abandon the battle, go and sleep in your warm beds, in the bosoms of your beloved wives, our children will damn us till doomsday. Do not compare the battle of Khirmanjig, which now waits us, to other battles. Do not remain motionless and do not turn your back on the enemy. Shame on the soldier who is stabbed in the back by the enemy, do not lose your compassion in the battle, have mercy on unarmed infants and the aged!

Do not insult or humiliate Armenian wives and children, do not torture them! If you commit such acts, then we shall be shamed in the presence of our generous prophet." With these words he loaded his rifle. "Well, brothers, be ready! The enemy approaches!" Thus he finished his speech.

By this time the Armenians were within range and began firing at the Muslims. The Muslim soldiers at first fired from their trenches and fortifications and broke up the orderly movement of the enemy. The Armenians preferred not to extend the battlefield, and the Muslim commanders ordered their soldiers to leave the trenches and attack. The infantry built new fortifications and sniper posts on the left and on the right, and began to press the enemy from both sides.

The Armenians, under pressure, divided their forces into three and began to fire at the Muslim infantry. The Muslim commanders in return increased the number of the infantry, adding a further 400 soldiers. The Armenians demonstrated their complete ignorance of the science of war. In response to the unexpected change in Muslim formations and sniper fire, they attacked with their cavalry. The Muslims opened fire from the centre and inflicted losses on the enemy. The Armenians understood their mistake, withdrew the cavalry and sent forward the infantry instead. The Muslim infantry immediately left their barricades and, shouting "Ya Allah, Ya Allah", immediately occupied the enemy's forward posititions. The Armenians totally lost their battle formation; the Muslims did not miss the opportunity and at once sent 100 infantry to hamper the enemy's withdrawal. Seeing this, the Armenians abandoned the battle and rushed back. They left a rearguard of about 30 cavalry. The roads being rocky and impassable, they were also obliged to give up their horses and flee to save their souls. The Muslims, aware of the mountainous terrain, began to pursue the enemy with their infantry.

The Armenian infantry and their horses could hardly make it through the narrow passages and assemble in the middle of the village; the Muslim snipers climbed the rocks like mountain goats and poured fire onto the village from all four sides. The Armenians could not find a way to mobilize their forces; they lost heart and were obliged to leave the village.

After occupying the village the Muslims looted and then set it on fire. The Armenians suffered great losses in this battle, but they preferred not to speak about it. When the village was burning and the Muslims were returning with their trophies, they fell into an Armenian ambush. As they had occupied favourable positions, 16 Muslims were killed. Then there was silence after the battle for several days. The government, as if from slumber, opened its eyes and hinted to the chief of the district to ask the Muslim Gazi for peace. When the Muslim aghsaggal* assembled and gave their consent to peace, the chief of the district sent a telegram to the Armenians and invited them to the village of Gezlek for peace talks. The next day he took the Muslim elders to the village of Kurd Mahmud, which is in the neighbourhood of the Muslim village of Gezlek and three versts from the Armenian habitations of Hadrut and Khunbabat *yuvasi***.

While the peace preparations were underway, the Muslim fighters were in the village of Kurd Mahmud, but did not appear in public because of a ban by the Muslim elders. The chief of the district had also gone to Hadrut. Taking advantage of the situation, the police chief of the second station in Hadrut, Davydov by name, attacked the village of Arish with guardsmen and an Armenian detachment. They set half of the village on fire and escaped. Two or three hours later the Muslims were invited to the village of Sarajig by the police chief of the district. In this way the Armenians and Muslims assembled in Sarajig, restored peace and agreed an armistice.

---

* *Aghsaggal* - Respectable, honourable, literally - white-bearded.
** *Yuva* - Nest.

The battle of Gishlag

A horse from the Armenian village of Surli went astray and joined the herd of the Muslim village of Gishlag. The Armenians cried out: "Hey, the Muslims have driven away our herd, stop them." So saying, they attacked the Muslim village with a detachment of volunteers and tried to drive away all the Muslims' herd. The Muslims heard about this and tried to resist. As the Armenians exceeded them in number, the Muslims, with the help of people from the village of Suleymen, pursued the enemy, but as the roads were rocky and impassable, the Muslims were defeated and the village of Gishlag was set on fire. It is believed that they suffered damage worth 7,000-8,000 manats. The residents of the destroyed village did not want to live like vagabonds, so they attacked the Armenian village of Dolanlar. Other Muslim volunteers came to help them and the Armenians were defeated, they lost ten men and left the village. The Muslims were short of battle supplies. A Muslim, dishonest and devoid of national pride, advised the Armenians: "Don't leave the battle, the Muslims will soon retreat." In this way he gave moral encouragement to the Armenians. The Muslims were obliged to retreat because of a lack of cartridges.

The battle of Mazraa

The following day, the Armenians mobilized their forces and attacked the village of Mazraa. As the residents of Mazraa had gone to the summer pastures, there were only nine guards in the village. After several hours of combat, six Muslims were killed and an old man was taken captive. Six Armenians were also killed. Muslims from nearby villages came to assist them. The battle continued for two days. The son of a man by the name of Tatar Hasan, from the village of Ahmedli, was killed in the battle. The Muslims took their wives and left the village.

The Armenians looted the village and set it on fire. We must also record that the village of Mazraa is surrounded by Armenian villages on all sides. As sufficient assistance did not arrive, the

Muslims were defeated there. We must also note that battles in this province began in March and continued until the tragedies in Shusha.

The latest news

Five days after the last tragedy in Shusha, news of the troubles and riots spread quickly. People everywhere began to make preparations to go to Shusha. In addition, 50 mounted residents of Shusha came from the direction of Agdam to march together towards their town. About 400 cavalry following the Molla Nasraddin road to Shusha were attacked by Armenians in an ambush at a spot called Khoshandam. The Muslims unsheathed their daggers and rushed into battle, the cavalry drove them to the Armenian village of Afshar and fought in the village for three hours. The Armenians could not withstand the resistance and began to flee. After the battle the Muslims decided to set out for Shusha, but as a man was killed in a quarrel among them, the cavalry scattered. As much has been written about the events in Shusha, we do not think it necessary to repeat it.

The last letters

After the events in Shusha, the cattle of the village of Garadagli in the district of Jabrail-Karyagin were driven away by Armenians. The residents rushed to tackle them and several Armenians were killed. The others scattered and ran away. Among those killed was an Armenian nationalist. This enraged his compatriots and they sent the chief of the district police, Davydov, to catch the murderer and deliver him to them.

The action taken by the pro-Armenian police chief Davydov

The chief of police advised them thus: "I shall go to the village of Garadagli and engage the villagers involved in discussion. You come and hide in the orchard. I shall send the murderer to the orchard. You can shoot and kill him there." In brief, the police chief sent the young man to the orchard in this way and the Armenians fired and wounded him. The poor man somehow managed to escape and rush into the village. Aware of this, the Armenians also ran from the site. The next day the Armenians gathered and again attacked the village of Garadagli. The Muslims could not hold out against the attack because of the large number of the enemy, and they left the village. The Armenians looted the village and the nearby Yukhari Gezlek, a village of 15 households.

Summary of events

The Armenians began fighting first. They attacked and destroyed the villages of Veisalli and Divanali in the district of Jabrail-Karyagin. A number of Armenian villages were also destroyed in this war. The villages of Avshar, Dudukchu, Akhullu, Agbulag, Khirmanjig, Dolanlar, Koshandam were among them. They also suffered not a few losses.

When the Muslims moved to the summer pastures, two winter pastures were destroyed by the Armenians. The town of Shusha was the main reason for the Armenians' defeat in this district, because the Armenians had collected their main forces in Shusha in order to totally wipe out the Muslims there. On the other hand, the Muslims of Jabrail were the best warriors and fought bravely, they shook the Armenians thoroughly. But the government did not stir to restore peace or establish an armistice in this district, although it had a good supply of arms and ammunition in Shusha. Goloshapov kept the government troops in Shusha in order to help the Armenians. As the last tragedy took place, not a single soldier was found in the district to restore peace.

Painful Events in Shusha, or the Wretchedness of Ignorance

Description of the events in the district of Shusha,
province of Ganja, which took place on 16 August 1905

If one examines closely the works and deeds, the mood and life of the Armenians of Shusha, it becomes clear that they had been making war preparations.

It was clearly apparent that they were preparing for a major confrontation, for a terrible event. It was obvious to all that they were collecting arms and ammunition every day, every month.

The Muslims of Shusha thought that the Armenians lacked bravery and courage, and did not believe that they would rise up against them. The Muslims thought that "the Armenians were fit for nothing but a little trade. They had no youth to take up arms and fight." Thinking this way, they ignored what the Armenians were doing; each was involved in his own work and concerns. In describing the lack of awareness among the Muslims of Shusha I think I will become a target for the hatred of readers. These noble people were brave and courageous from birth, but to introduce them to readers as ignorant and unaware of world affairs is worthy of contempt, is it not?! After putting onto paper the events in Shusha, I thought it necessary to say a few kind words about them.

There is no need to criticise the words of the correspondent about the noble feelings of the Muslims of Shusha, nevertheless, to attribute this purity of heart and nobility of feeling to their ignorance is a mistake, I cannot but think of it like that. On the other hand, I also want to write a few words about the ignorance of the residents of Shusha in order to cool the passions attached to our criticism of the correspondent. The following are my brief notes about the ignorance of the Muslims of Shusha, to which I wish to draw readers' attention.

Before the painful Armenian-Muslim events took place in the Caucasus, the Muslims received information from newspapers and magazines about the Armenians, who are very industrious, but few in number, and who started a row every week somewhere in the country.

When the Muslims heard about the massacre of Armenians in Istanbul in Turkey, about the tragedies in Sasun and Zeytun, they said "the Armenians are not guilty in this, the crime originated in Turkish fanaticism."

What confused these native Muslims was the deceptively superficial love expressed by the Armenians to the Muslims for peace and order. On the other hand, the ridiculous saying "An Armenian can never be a warrior", passed down from Muslim ancestors, was misguided advice to their successors.

Time passed, year succeeded year, the Muslims opened their eyes and saw that in some places, in Russia for instance, the Armenians were engaged in war preparations day and night. The Muslims were surprised and astonished and were plunged into thought. This quality was also inherent to the Muslims of Shusha. The Armenians began to speak very sweetly to them, as they did in Iran and Turkey, to gain more profitable employment. First they began to say: we are making preparations, not for fighting against Muslims or other nations, but to achieve autonomy within Russia." And the Muslims believed this nonsense and continued with their own affairs. Bravo!!

My thoughts

The Muslims of Shusha were deceived by the Armenians' corrosive dreams of autonomy and did nothing towards their own defence or military preparation. To write about this and disclose the essence of their strivings is not a waste of time. If the Armenians achieve autonomy, or something similar, will all the nations of the

Caucasus be equally represented in it, will the Armenians be considered equal and enjoy equal rights with other Caucasian nations? No, no, they will not. The intention of the Armenians is not to achieve autonomy, but to build an independent Armenian state, which is only a dream and cannot be realized. If the Armenians achieve autonomy, other nations of the Caucasus will be subjected to oppression. Would the Muslims reconcile themselves to such oppression, I wonder? Or would our Georgian brothers, who are stronger than us, who set out on the path of progress before us, accept such oppression and humiliation?!

Doubtless, neither the Georgians nor we have the desire or patience to become an oppressed nation due to Armenian egoism.

In such circumstances it was necessary for the Georgians and for us to make preparations. Now let us see! Will Russian autocracy view the inconceivable ambitions of the Armenians in silence?!

No! No! It will not. It will repel the stones flung at it from all sides and give the necessary response, however weak it is. It is as clear as day that when repulsing those stones, they may damage one of the Caucasian nations. As the proverb says "A bludgeon hits only a friend"; those stones will hit the Muslims, of that there is no doubt. This means that the Russian government will abstain from confrontation with the Armenians, but will make one of the Muslim nations face them. And we shall be that nation, because we are the most underdeveloped of the Caucasian nations in education and knowledge. Proof of my words is the declaration that "the government is guilty in this," which often appears in the Caucasian and Russian press. However, we must not only blame the government, but also the Armenians and their barbarous parties. When all is said and done, we must conclude that the Muslims should have made preparations in due time, taken the measures necessary for their defence and not tolerated the insults and humiliations. This was the basic and necessary duty of the Muslims. But they did not think about it. The events in Nakhchivan were the result. These events awakened some Muslim provinces and the Muslims of Shusha. When the Armenians understood this, they again began to speak smoothly and in a sweet, flattering manner: "Well, brothers, we have been brother nations in the same motherland for many years. We had nothing to do with the fighting in Nakhchivan, or Baku. We are again brothers." In short, such sweet words lulled back to sleep the Muslims who were just about to wake up. At the same time, the Armenians oppressed the Muslims in some villages, killing and robbing them whenever they had the chance. It continued like this until the August of 1905. At 2 o'clock at night on 8 August, on the corner of the street which separated the Armenian and Muslim quarters, an Iranian Muslim, whose duty was to light and extinguish the street lanterns, was killed by Armenians. Once again seeds of conflict were sown between the two nations.

Painful information about the riots, or Muslim successes

At the time, date and place detailed above several Armenians attacked an Iranian and killed him. Although people reached him at his last breath, it was in vain, the criminals had escaped. This brutal crime excited the Muslims very much, but supporters of peace restored security and prevented riots. Again in those days, over three hundred armed Armenians attacked a peaceful nomad caravan of Muslims near the Armenian village of Veng, killing and robbing them. This news made the Muslims very bitter; there were other potential causes of riots, however, the peace commission managed to contain the situation. On 16 August, at 9 o'clock in the morning, in the Armenian cemetery adjoining the Muslim graveyard, the Cossacks made an attempt to disarm an Armenian, but he did not obey their order and resisted, as a result he was killed. Although there were witnesses that he had been killed by the Cossacks, the Armenians accused the Muslims of the murder and had a pretext for riots. They began to violate order in the city, in the bazaar and in the streets. The dentist Mashoryans, instructed by Armenian intelligence, began to deliver speeches at rallies and call the people to rebel. He invented various stories to incite people to disorder. He also spread such information as "this hour news has come in that four Armenians have been brutally killed near the Muslim village of Zarisli." As soon as the Armenians heard the news, the troubles began. The church bell called the Armenians to the church.

The disseminators of the news about the murder of the Armenians, Mashoryans and his friends Atabeyov and Dolkhanov, quickly mounted their horses and galloped to the quarter of the town called the Gate of Irevan, as if to learn more about the Armenians murdered in the village of Zarisli and then return. The Armenians in the church soon returned home, collected their arms, went to their shops and waited for the start of the riot. At this point those who had gone to bring news returned to the town with an Armenian who had fallen from his horse and was injured. This bleeding man was displayed in every corner to the crowd of Armenians, saying: "Do you see what the Muslims are doing to us?" It was a signal to begin the riots. The Armenians watching this scene were very much impressed and excited, they killed a Muslim by the name of Gara who was making his way through the bazaar.

The flames of riot soon spread all over the town. This time a porter from Iran, a Muslim, was murdered. After these events the Armenians attacked the Muslims in the Armenian bazaar, who were unaware of what was going on, and began to murder them, using all kinds of weapons. Khosrov bey Fuladov was charged with investigating the tragedy in Zarisli, he was also fired at by Armenians while fulfilling his duty. On that day the Armenians murdered or wounded most of the Muslims who happened to be there with them. Rifles showered fire on people from trenches and barriers prepared in advance, and also from the Armenian church. They attempted to shoot Muslims from the roofs of houses.

The Muslims who witnessed this heartbreaking scene murdered the Armenians who happened to be in the Muslim bazaar. They also took several Armenians home for the sake of security. As soon as the riots began, a Muslim quarter neighbouring on an Armenian quarter was attacked. An Armenian murdered the son of his Muslim neighbour Abbas bey, his brother and several of his servants. Then the Muslims of the quarter began to murder all the Armenians there and set fire to their houses. On the first day of the riot the Muslims were in confusion and reflection, they simply tried to defend themselves. But the Armenians did their utmost to torture the Muslims, and were reluctant to cease firing for a moment. When the riots began, 15 Armenian soldiers armed with rifles ran from their barracks and came to help the Armenians.

16 August 1905

The events of 17 August 1905

At dawn the Armenians resumed their barbarism, setting on fire eight Muslim houses in the Kocharli quarter and murdering their inhabitants. Again came very painful news that in the Khalfali quarter, in the Armenian sector, ten houses had been burnt and their inhabitants murdered. Several soldiers from the barracks were sent to help the Muslims who had been the victims of betrayal. The Armenians killed two of the soldiers and prevented the rest from protecting the Muslims.

Seeing such aggressive and brutal behaviour from the Armenians, Muslim youth ignored the advice of the chiefs and clerics of the town and launched an all-out attack on the Armenians. This terrorized and confused them, because the Muslims set on fire all the places they occupied.

The Armenians had the most up-to-date arms, nevertheless, they could not withstand the attacks for a moment, displaying neither endurance or courage. Their losses horrified them and they tried to leave the battlefield as soon as possible. The bloody battle continued from the early morning until late in the evening. It illustrated the victory and bravery of the Muslims, at the same time confounding other nations, who could not utter anything but praise for the Muslims.

The Armenians could not hold their trenches, which resembled those used in the defence of the castle of Port-Arthur[*] in the Russia-

---

[*] Port-Arthur, fortress (the present city of Lyushun, China). During the Russian-Japanese war Port Arthur collapsed and surrendered to Japan.

Japan war of 1904, and were forced to evacuate. When they did so, they encountered fire from the Muslim volunteers and fell dead or wounded in front of their own trenches. The scene was one of horror and barbarity. The number of Armenians dying from heart attacks through fear exceeded the number of those killed by fire and dagger. In this battle, while Muslim volunteers numbered one thousand, there were ten times more Armenians. When the Armenians left the trenches and took to their heels, not pausing for a moment, the Muslims began to pursue and kill them as soon as they got hold of them. No shred of mercy remained in the hearts of Muslims for the Armenians, because the Muslims had begged them many times for peace, but without result.

17 August 1905

The events of 18 August 1905

On this day the Armenians rallied their forces and renewed the fighting. They again suffered physical and moral destruction and lost many people killed. The Muslims outgunned them, deceived them with many ruses, fired at them from all sides and set their quarters on fire. The Armenians were utterly routed. They had wanted to take revenge for the previous day, but suffered great losses and left their quarters to the Muslims.

18 August 1905[19]

---

[19]There were such bloody clashes on this day that the correspondent did not have sufficient time to describe everything in detail. He calls 18 August the bloody day of Shusha. On this day the Muslims fought very bravely. On this day, while the battle raged, a Muslim climbed the minaret of a mosque and appealed to people thus:"Men! Poor is the Muslim if on this day of battle he plunders anything from an Armenian, or stretches his hand to stain the honour of an Armenian lady who is being trampled by the Muslims."

The events of 19 August 1905

On the fourth day of fighting the Muslims defeated the Armenians, burned and destroyed their shops and houses. Among the buildings burnt in the war were the Khandemirov Theatre, the School for Girls, the office of the Court of Justice and many other famous buildings.

The Armenians had never suffered so much in previous struggles as on that day. They showed their fear and rushed into the barracks like a flock of sleep to escape from the Muslims. Although the Armenians were armed and outnumbered the Muslims four to one, most preferred to leave the town and scatter in all four directions. The youth of Hayastan[*], who was once frightening in appearance, now with a wine skin on his back, four cartridge-belts around his waist and a repeater rifle on his shoulder, hid himself under a bed in the soldiers' barracks and believed his life worth more than the humiliation suffered. On that day the members of various Armenian parties abandoned the trenches, only a dozen old and disabled men were left there, knowing that they were not able to fight. The Muslims drove these old and disabled men from the trenches and ensured their security, because the Muslim elders and commanders had ordered the Muslims in advance not to use arms against the aged or children.

At the height of the Muslims' victory the Armenian Archimandrite and Governor Baranovsky went to the yard of the mosque. The Archimandrite begged the Muslims in this way:

"Muslims, have mercy! We know that the Armenians are guilty of this war in Shusha, but none remain here. Now only a handful of old, disabled, poor and miserable Armenians are still here, pity them, have mercy on them! Shedding tears, he implored them for peace. The Muslims stopped the battle and the firing ceased. But the Armenians again violated the peace, they fired at the governor on his way home. On that day the Muslims remained peaceful and did not engage in any aggression.

19 August 1905

---

[*] i.e. Armenia.

The events of 20 August 1905

On this day the Armenians again violated the ceasefire and continued to fire at the Muslims. Such impudent behaviour enraged the Muslim youth, therefore they launched a frontal attack. They marched to the Armenian Square in the town, heedless of anything and thinking of nothing. Frightened by the charge, the Armenians fired canons several times and exploded several grenades. But they could not stop the enraged Muslim youth. This continued until everybody was sure that it was the end of the Armenians in Shusha. At just this moment, several Armenian clerics, government officials with Bibles and church banners in their hands, with crosses over their heads, proceeded to the mosque to a mournful musical march and with several soldiers. They hoisted one of the banners on the minaret of the mosque to warn the Armenians to stop firing during peace negotiations. The government officials and the chief of police begged and pleaded with the Muslims to pardon the Armenians. The Muslims accepted their armistice proposal once again. But when they left the mosque yard to go home, a Muslim was killed by a shot from the Armenian barrier. The Muslims displayed patience and did not violate the conditions of peace. The Armenians maintained fierce fire from their houses until the evening.

20 August 1905

The events of 21 August 1905

On this day the Muslims took the Armenians sheltered in their houses and delivered them to the Armenian elders and authorities. The Armenians released only five or six Muslims. Several days later the Armenians beheaded 17 Iranian workers who had been repairing a school called Realniy. In this way they again aggrieved and upset the Muslims. The Muslims did not take revenge upon these dishonest and brutal Armenians, preferring to maintain peace. After the ceasefire it became clear that all the Armenian shops located in the Muslim quarter had remained safe and untouched. But all the Muslim shops in the Armenian quarter had been looted

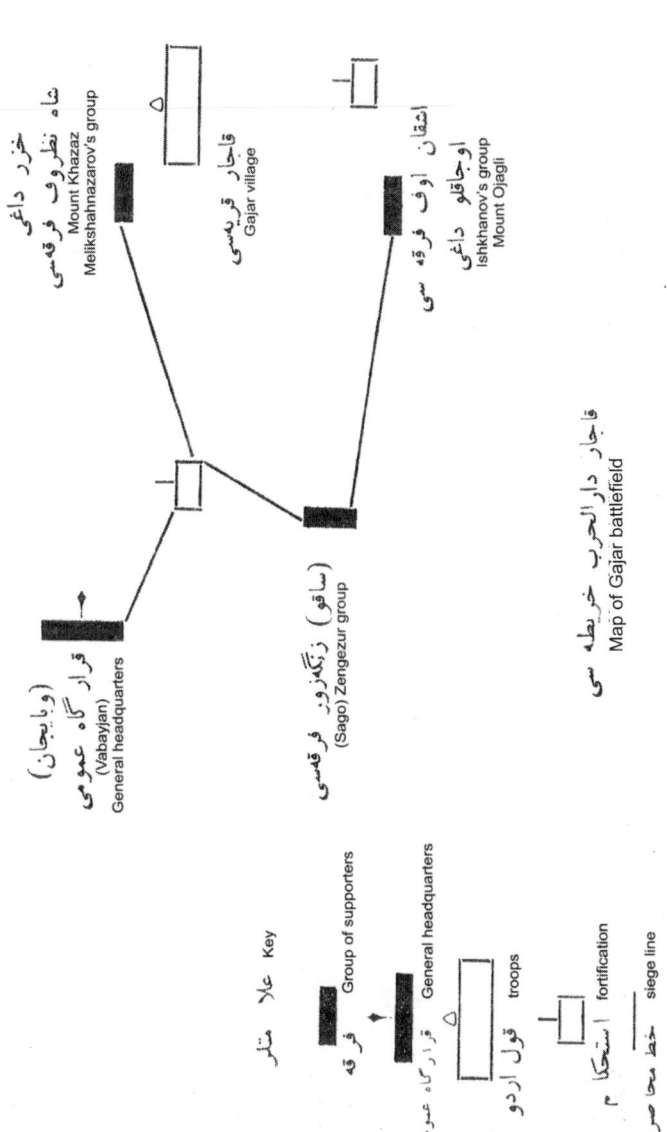

and destroyed. Muslim losses in the clashes were 100 killed and wounded, not more. The Armenians always hid their losses, but this time Muslim volunteers counted the corpses and the Armenians could not hide the facts.

20 Muslim houses were burnt in the clashes in Shusha, the Armenians also lost many houses and shops destroyed and burnt.

Thus the fighting, which began on 16 August, ended with the declaration of peace on 21August. In these hostilities, the Armenian soldiers were closely supported by their own nation. But the government remained neutral.

The correspondent's report has remained unchanged.
21 August 1905.

Second Tragedy in Shusha, or Goloshapov's Deception

Details of the tragedy brought about in the town of Shusha, province of Ganja, on 12 July 1905, by Goloshapov's deception.

Expression of intent

From the first Armenian-Muslim conflicts and clashes in the district of Shusha in Ganja province to the final tragedies, many governors general were appointed to the district. A little before the latest tragedy, General Goloshapov was again appointed Governor General of Shusha. It may be said that he applied a new method of administration and revealed his true nature with every month that passed.

The Governors General Tagashvili, Fleisher and Goloshapov, who succeeded each other to the post, were more interested in orgies, drinking and feasting than in the affairs of the district. They never displayed any interest in the work and did not exert themselves. The only thing they tried to do was to gain the consent of both sides and to win the sympathy of one or other of the sides by various strategems.

General Goloshapov seemed simple and pure-hearted at first sight, but in reality he was cunning and ruthless. When he was appointed to Shusha and left for Karabagh he said in public: "The Armenians will kill me, I hope I am killed by dagger or pistol, because I am afraid of being blown up by a bomb."

When he first arrived in Shusha, he lived in the Muslim quarter and his goal was to draw the Muslims to his side. He was recalled from Shusha several times for falsifying investigations into Armenian-Muslim cases. This was a time when the government dreamed of keeping the Caucasus stable and balanced.

This was why Goloshapov was recalled and substituted by Alftan.

Being very artful, Goloshapov managed to get a letter of agreement from the Armenian and Muslim representatives and left for Tiflis (now Tbilisi, the residence of the viceroy of the Russian emperor). Alftan treated both nations equally and very often fined, punished or reproached Armenian villages which committed crimes and acts of barbarism.

When the Armenians understood that such a man would be of no use to them, they resorted to new schemes. First of all, the cleric of the church in Shusha wrote eloquent and impressive letters to the Empress and to Duchess Vorontsova on behalf of Armenian women, then, by deception, he got a letter from the Muslim and Armenian representatives giving their consent to Goloshapov's re-appointment to Shusha. Then the Armenians began to accuse General Alftan, an honest man, of things he had never done, trying to discredit him in the eyes of the government. For instance, they began to spread the calumny that "General Alftan is disgracing young girls and elderly women in the villages, stop him, we beg you". They continued that "if Goloshapov is not appointed and General Alftan, with his accomplices Lieutenant-Colonel Vevren, chief of police of the district Frelikh, and others do not leave Shusha, the Armenians will live in misery and trouble henceforward."

The viceroy read the letters and sent his deputy with several interrogators to examine the case; after investigation it became clear that the persons mentioned in the said letters were very fair and not guilty of anything. He was obliged to have two governors general in the province of Ganja and so General Alftan was charged with ruling one part of the province, General Goloshapov the other. The latter made two trips to Karabagh, but did not even give Javanshir, Zengezur and Jabrail a glance. He focused his main attention on the district of Shusha.

Goloshapov's actions

When General Goloshapov came to Shusha for the second time, four Muslims were shot by Armenians in Askeran while they were carting fruit. Some other Muslims were murdered while they were watering their orchards. When the Muslims went to the police to complain about the murders, Goloshapov was there, too. He said the following words to them, very clearly:

"Crimes committed off the roads, that is, places which are not public paths or highways, are not at my disposal, they are outside my responsibility."

With these words he returned to his house. Some time later several Armenian meliks (noblemen) were killed on their way from Yevlakh to Shusha and some men were taken captive. In this case the brave Goloshapov fined the village of Shiklar 2000 roubles. Then Muslim robbers killed an Armenian policeman in the district of Gorus. This Goloshapov had a Muslim noblemen of Shusha by the name of Najafgfulu Aga arrested and put in prison for three months, on the basis of false information against him from a group of Armenians.

At this time Armenians blocked the road in Askeran and cut Shusha's communications with the province completely. This was done to prevent the Muslims from receiving assistance from anywhere.

News of the war

After the closure of the road in Askeran, the Muslims could only get assistance from the village of Zarisli and other Muslim villages in the west. Troops and artillery were sent several times to destroy them. But as the Muslims were well-defended, the combined Russian-Armenian troops returned disappointed with their guns and artillery.

The final conflict. Troops launch cannon-fire at the fortress

The Armenians were aware that General Goloshapov disliked the Muslims. They were continually seeking pretexts to turn the General against them. They used different ploys for this purpose. In some cases they managed to achieve their ends, but in others they tried in vain because of the sober-mindedness and vigilance of the Muslims. Finally, on 12 July 1905, the Armenians displayed a male corpse, dead for several several days, to the General and said: "Look at him, he has just been killed in your neighbourhood - before you arrived." The General did not do anything to investigate the incident and, as he was looking for a pretext to settle accounts with the Muslims, he ordered cannons to be fired at the Muslim Kocharli quarter.

On the same day, detachments of Cossack and infantry from one side, and about 10,000 armed Armenian volunteers, regular soldiers, party members and robbers from another side, marched against the Muslims. The battle continued for five days. All the Muslim houses on the front line were burned and destroyed by artillery fire.

Young Muslim volunteers, although they did not get help from any direction, fought as desperately as Rustem in Firdausi's "Shahnameh." The Russian troops and Armenians fired shrapnel at the Muslims from their cannons. The Muslim volunteers were not able to answer the enemy cannon fire, nevertheless they were not discouraged, they did not retreat a single step, firing volleys at the enemy positions from rifles which gradually grew in number.

The Armenians suffered great losses. Confident in their own strength they frequently left their trenches and attacked the Muslims. The latter met them bravely with fire, did not let them advance a single step and scattered them. Recognising the Armenians' grave situation, General Goloshapov ordered his remaining troops to join the battle. On the fifth day of fighting an all-out attack was launched against the Muslims.

Alongside the cannons, about 6,000 rifles fired simultaneously at the Muslim positions. Maintaining their fire, the Muslims retreated to their last line of defence. At the height of the battle one of the Muslim commanders encouraged the fighters to attack their own trenches, now occupied by the Armenians and Cossacks. The Muslims, aged from seven to seventy, marched against the enemy positions bearing their arms. The Armenians and Cossacks could not resist such a flood of Muslim fighters, who kept up an incessant barrage. The enemy was obliged to retreat.

The Muslims drove the Armenians to their houses and the Cossacks to their headquarters. The Armenian volunteers found refuge in the wilderness by taking to their heels. There remained only the Muslim martyrs and volunteers, who struck the final blow against the Armenians who were unable to flee and who hid close to the battlefield. The latter dragged away as many bodies as they could, but they were scattered across the ground like leaves in autumn. They littered the battlefield and were trampled by the Muslim volunteers chasing the enemy.

General Goloshapov was a witness to the Muslims' victory and the defeat of his supporters. He withdrew to his house and did not stir from there. But before then he had stood on a hilltop and watched the battle. He saw the Muslim victory and also how they fired at several Armenian houses. The houses burned out completely, the flames threatening neighbouring buildings, but the heavy rain which had begun to fall soon prevented that.

On the sixth day of fighting, that is on 18 July, General Goloshapov assembled representatives from both sides and came to the Muslim quarter of the town to hear their views. While talking to the Muslims he wept and said: "Just for an armistice, you made a real war out of a trifle."[20]

18 July 1906

The latest news

After all this, after so much cannon fire and shrapnel, particularly after such a fierce battle with government troops and a thousand Dashnak detachments, the Muslims had suffered great damage to their property, nevertheless their human losses were a tenth of those suffered by the other side. The Muslims had 30 men killed, they happened to be people uninvolved in the battle. The Armenians witheld information about their losses. But according to the

---

[20] When General Goloshapov wept and hypocritically dabbed his eyes with a handkerchief while talking to the Muslims, it reminded me of the following lines by Hafiz Shirazi, the Persian poet:"You murdered Hafiz yourself and are also mourning him."

Russians in Khankendi, about 400 bodies had been carried away from the town. The number of bodies hidden in the town remained unknown.

Several Cossacks who had taken part in the battle on the Armenian side were also killed. On 18 July, peace and the armistice were restored. The Armenians and the government troops had witnessed the Muslims' bravery. This time they would not have begun fighting had they not been able to rely on government troops. They had never imagined that the Muslims would forget the saying "a soldier is coming, run away", and be ready to defend their rights. We hope that henceforward our Armenian neighbours will not be deceived by the government and their politicians, and will not add a further dark page of disappointment to their history. As for General Goloshapov, the bitter taste of regret will never leave him until he drinks from the goblet of mortality.

Our people will also not forget that in the second battle of Shusha, Muslim males from seven to seventy took to arms. While the battles continued, the women were carrying ammunition and food to the trenches and barricades. By carrying bread, water and other necessities to their fighters, these women, who had never left their houses, won the sympathy and congratulations of the whole world. May God bless them. We beg God Almighty to let them bear the soldiers of the future and to raise them properly. "A soldier's mother is also a soldier", said our ancestors. We pray to God, asking for God's blessings on them and end our narration.

Sudden Onset of Tragedy in Baku

On 20 August, at 5:30 on a Saturday evening, when the young volunteer Muslim defenders were not in the city, there was a sudden attack.

The Muslims suffered great losses; those suffering most were the porters, workers from Iran and cart drivers. The Muslims had been unaware of the Armenians' military preparations. In addition, I think they had regarded the defeat of the Armenians on 6 February as a final victory. Had they thought of doing anything bad to the Armenians, they would not have left the town and gone to their summer houses and summer pastures, leaving the city at the disposal of the porters, cart-drivers and cabmen. And the Armenians would never have dared rise against the Muslims, had they been in the city.

There is no need to prove this. Both Armenians and Muslims thought that the Armenians had been morally defeated during February's tragedy and had not yet revived their forces. Thus they would not be able to renew hostilities.

The events of 20 August seemed to be a blessing to the Armenians. Their dreams and deeds suddenly took control of their souls and stirred them to attack the Muslims at night, when the city was completely empty and defenceless.

Details of the trouble

Several days before the second tragedy in Baku, the horse tramway workers had gone on strike. They did this because of their low wages. And instead of meeting their demands the government replaced the drivers with soldiers, putting them to work. This enraged the drivers further.

The striking drivers and their office workers were mostly Armenians. Displeased with the government's response they fired at horse-trams on the Saturday. As a result soldiers and several Muslim passengers on the horse-trams were killed or wounded.

Exploiting this opportunity, the Armenian church rang its bells. The Armenian youth standing in front of the shops clapped their hands, giving the signal to the shopkeepers to begin the troubles. The shopkeepers began to fire at Muslims, killing cart drivers, a waterman and others engaged in their daily work on the streets.

The Armenians began military-style riots against the Muslims all over the city. They fired continuously on Muslims from their house windows. They also fired at Russians and Georgians without distinction. We should also mention that they wanted to take revenge for the February events.

Information on the riot by Yegintin, chief of police of the Fourth Quarter

The Armenians began the riot in Parapet, near the Armenian church, by ringing the church bells as a signal. Within a few minutes the Armenians were firing bullets at Muslims in the street from the windows and balconies of their houses. In some places they attacked Muslims in their houses and shops, committing murder and looting.

Despite a government ban, the Armenians set houses on fire, where the owners were not at home, and barbarously destroyed shops and store-houses. The Muslims were not able to resist them; they were unarmed and had no military training. Shots were fired from the following Armenian houses: Mikhailov's Charity House and the houses of Osipov, Yegizarov, Avakov, Mayilov, Antonov and Adamov. At night rifles and pistols were fired at government troops and police from the windows of the Charity House and the houses of Antonov, Mayilov and Yegizarov. Again, according to information from the same police chief, the reason for all this was the Armenians' national crusade - they had been making preparations for some time.

Written report from police chief Eizbash

Everything began at the base of the Third Cossack Regiment, from the old Labinsky Regiment, the Sixth Artillery and the Fire-Fighter Regiments. On 21 August, Armenian residents of houses located on the road leading to the palace in Icheri-sheher (Old City) fired at the positions of the Cossacks and the artillerymen. Sixteen Cossacks and several artillerymen who happened to be in the barracks, with the help of the 82nd Dagestan Regiment, responded to the Armenians. The window panes and walls of the barracks resembled a honeycomb after the shooting. Bullets fell like hail into the yard.

The crockery and other articles in the rooms of the soldiers and the commander were smashed to pieces. The commander declared that the soldiers' room had been hit by a storm of fire. The traces of 284 rifle and 7 pistol bullets were counted on the walls of the house where the soldiers lived. When the chief of police ordered the breaking down of the doors of houses from which the Armenians had fired, they found nobody there, everybody had escaped. The Russians living there stated that there had been many Armenians and all of them had been firing. When the houses were searched, two pistols, six daggers, 100 cartridges and three repeater rifles were found and taken. When the chief of police was returning to his office, he was fired on by some Armenians; fortunately, they did not hit him.

News of 21 August

The supervisors of Baku's Fourth Quarter unanimously reported that on 21 August, at 5 o'clock in the evening, they were fired on from Bagirov's house in Krasnovodskaya Street but, fortunately, nobody was wounded.

On 25 August several shots were fired from the balcony of the same house facing Surakhanskaya Street. A Turk was wounded as a result. The second time that shots were fired from the door of the same house, the soldiers fired back. The result is not known but, later, there was further firing from the house. The supervisors of the quarter said that Bagirov's house had been a trap for the police and military.

Information delivered by Yegintin, chief of police of the Fourth Quarter of Baku

On 15 August 1905, a company of soldiers from the Dagestan Regiment, commanded by non-commissioned officer Tekhmichenko, captured 47 Armenians and brought them to Baku's Fourth Police Station and declared that they had assembled in the house of Kudikov and had fired at ordinary people and government clerks who were passing in phaetons or on foot. Therefore, by order of Captain Dubrovin, they broke into the house in order to capture the miscreants. As a result of their search, they found several Berdan rifles, revolvers and cartridges. All the arms and ammunition were delivered to the police station.

By order of Captain Inozemsev, a senior non-commissioned officer of the same regiment took a company of soldiers and conducted searches of the houses of Varshapetov and Mammadrza Rasulbeyov located in Magazinnaya Street. This was done because people in the street had been fired on from these houses. They captured several men in these houses with many rifles and pistols, and all were delivered to the captain.

61 trouble-makers were captured, but as the prison was full, the prison chief did not take them in.

Announcement by the chief of the port

The next day the chief of the sea port declared to the chief of city police that on 24 August the watchman of the port office, Savili Mukhnatkin, had told him that at 5.30 am. four pistol shots had been fired from the balcony of the house of Adamov located at the junction of Merkurevskaya and Milutinskaya Streets. Fortunately, nobody had been killed or wounded and the watchmen could show and prove that he had been fired at from that balcony. At 11 o'clock Muslim passers-by had been fired at by rifles through the glass of a closed door to that house. On Saturday 20 August, many shots were fired from the shops on the first floor of the house belonging to the Sergeyev Brothers, Mirzayans and Parutchiyev, and shots were also fired from Sasun's restaurant. On 20 August, there was shooting from the house facing

Avsharov's shop. The watchman of Avsharov's shop killed a man who lit street lamps. The port medical attendant Laktenov, watchman Mukhnatkin and the office clerk of the marine school witnessed the murder. Several Muslims were killed by shots from the Armenian houses located in Birjevaya Street behind the Post-Telegraph Office. The soldiers on guard in the street were also fired at from those houses and so the houses were besieged by the soldiers, but they could not break into them. By order of the officer of the day, the soldiers fired at the houses from the balconies of houses facing them, as a result, six Armenians and a Georgian were killed.

Report of Yegintin, chief of police of the Fourth Quarter

On 20 August, at 5 o'clock in the afternoon, Armenians opened fire at passers-by with rifles and pistols from open windows and casements. As a result, a Russian was killed in front of the house of Safaraliyev, at the junction of Morskaya and Torgovaya Streets, a Muslim phaeton driver was murdered in Stanislavskaya Street. In Balakhanskaya Street a Muslim was tortured to death and taken to Mikhailovsky Hospital.

On 21 August, a skirmish began at dawn and continued until 3 o'clock in the afternoon. After 3 o'clock the skirmishing was less intensive. The Armenians opened fire from the windows of their houses and gates at mounted and pedestrian Muslims. Four Muslims were murdered, three were wounded. Two Armenians were wounded and one was killed. The wounded were taken to Mikhailovsky Hospital. The unidentified Muslim bodies were sent to the cemetery. The owners of the houses whence shots were fired were identified and interrogated.

On the night of 22 August, Armenians broke into grocery stores belonging to Iranian Muslims and looted them. The following stores were affected:

1. The grocery of Agadadash Bakhtiyev in the house of Dovletov, at the junction of Balakhani and Kaspi Streets.

2. The grocery of Seyid Dadash oglu in the house of Zeynalov, at

the junction of Telefonnaya and Kaspi Streets.

3. The grocery of an unknown Iranian in the house of Aliyev in Balakhanskaya Street.

4. The grocery of Mcshcdi Mustafa oglu in the house of Dadashov in Telefonnaya Street.

5. The grocery of Jafar Nasrullayev in the house of Safaraliyev in Bolshoy Morskaya Street.

The names of the Armenians caught red-handed were submitted to the local police station.

6. At 11 o'clock on 24 August, at 11, Ashurbey Street, 28 trouble-makers destroyed and looted the house of Shahnazarov. The perpetrators were arrested.

7. Again, at 25, Ashurbey Street the house of Alexandr Terasayev was set on fire and burnt out completely.

8. At 7 o'clock in the morning on 24 August, at the junction of Bolshoy Morskaya and Gimnazicheskaya Streets, two men were found wounded, with very little sign of life.

9. At the junction of Surakhanskaya and Bazarnaya Streets a Russian by the name of Yuri Antonovich was murdered.

10. In front of the house at 29, First Capitan Street, a Muslim aged 55-60 was murdered.

11. In Bagirov's garden, policeman № 207, by the name of Hasanov, who was on guard in the Primorsky quarter, was fired at from a balcony by three Armenians near the house of Bagirov.

Report of the chief of police of the Fourth Quarter on the events of 20-25 August

From 20-24 August, at 221, Karantinnaya Street, shots were fired randomly at passers-by from the balcony of the fourth floor of the house of the Filiposyans Brothers. Therefore, at 11 o'clock on 24 August, government troops fired at this house with cannons, destroying the interior and the walls of the fourth floor. Subsequently, nobody returned fired from this building.

There were no further tragedies on the following days in the Fourth Quarter.

On 26 August, at 10 o'clock at night, two Armenian criminals broke into the shop of Jafar Mirbaba oglu in Ter-Petrosyan's house in Telefonnaya Street. When deputy chief of police Lazarev and military police approached, they fired at them. As a result, one of the criminals escaped, the other, Artem Semyonov by name, was caught.

On 26 August, Nikolay Akopov, an Armenian serving in the Fourth Quarter, was caught. Together with his Armenian accomplices he had attempted to loot the goods cart of a man named Ahmad Bagirov who came from Balakhani.

On 26 August, Armenians fired 25 shots and wounded Farid Abdul Zeynal oglu in Balakhanskaya Street in the house of Mayilov. One of the Armenians, by the name of Sergey Nalbandov, was arrested. The greatest damage was believed to have been suffered by the oil fields in Balakhani, Baku. In the troubles, which began on 20 August and continued until September 1905, many crimes were committed in Baku and its suburbs. The prices of goods rose threefold, poor people and migrants were driven into great need and poverty.

On 10 September, Count Vorontsov-Dashkov came to Baku to restore peace and the armistice. Peace was restored on 14 September, led by Viceroy Vorontsov-Dashkov.

The conditions of peace

On Thursday 14 September 1905, at about 12 o'clock, a crowd of Armenians and Muslims, over one thousand in number, with noblemen and clerics of both nations in attendance, assembled in Duma Square to settle peace and an armistice. The crowd seemed to be merry and content, and they accepted the peace proposal from the clerics. The Gazi of the province, Mir Muhammad Kerim aga Mir Jafarzade, invited the people to establish peace.

Then the Armenian cleric and the Governor General[*] gave advice to the crowd. To the sound of music, the crowd walked to Parapet,

---

[*] According to the author, the Governor of the Baku Province was V.V.Alishevskiy (1905-1915).

then from Kolubakinskaya Street towards Morskaya and Telefonnaya Streets. Then they returned to Stanislavskaya and Balakhanskaya Streets, and to Guba Meydani.* There were several other groups of people in the square. The cleric and popular residents of the city delivered impressive speeches and summoned people to peace. The crowd was led by Lieutenant-General Fadeyev and Governor-General Lileyev on a phaeton. The residents of the city were cheerful and merry. The streets and pavements were full of people. Armenians and Muslims, hand-in-hand, full of joy and happiness, streamed onto the streets. If a man, on seeing such a merry crowd, claimed not to be amazed, then he does not know what merriment is.

Merriment was everywhere, everybody beamed with joy. The music playing for peace in Guba Meydani spread to the pavements, from there to the balconies, and from the balconies it rose to heaven.

The crowd was so joyful that they stroked the horses pulling the general's phaeton. They accompanied him to his house cheering and happy.

The Governor General rose to his feet on the phaeton and appealed to the crowd thus:

"Dear citizens! Today I am living the happiest day of my life. I shall never forget this day. Gentlemen! You must never forget this day. I wish you always to live in peace and truce!"

Then the Governor shook hands with people in the crowd and entered his house. Several persons were dispatched to convey the news to the country. Among them were head of department Kamil Safaraliyev and chief of Baku police Lieutenant Eizbash. The achievement of peace comforted the residents, they felt relieved. Trade and the former prices of goods were restored. May God make this peace eternal.

Newspaper *Heyat*,** №53-67

---

* Square.

** *Heyat* (Life) - daily socio-political, economic and literary newspaper in the Azerbaijani language. Printed in Baku from 7 June 1905 to 3 September 1906.

Scream of the Motherland

This concerns the biography and death of our great martyr Muhammadgulu bey Kengerli, killed on 29 August 1905, during Armenian-Muslim clashes in the town of Batumi by members of the Armenian Committee. The information which we convey to readers has been taken from letters sent by a correspondent and ordinary people, and edited to suit the taste and understanding of readers.

Explanation

On 29 August 1905, in the town of Batumi, Muhammadgulu bey Kengerli, a very popular man in the region, was brutally murdered by terrorists sent by the Armenian Committee. No Muslim living in the Caucasus could withhold his tears when he heard the news of his death. This man was ready to sacrifice his life for his motherland and nation. We thought it necessary to write his biography and leave it for his children and motherland. It was written and published in the 71st edition of the newspaper *Heyat* under the pen name *Shua*[*]. The newspaper has since ceased publication. After the publication of this article by *Shua*, I followed him, collected information from his article and from letters by friends of the deceased, selected and published this scream of the motherland.

All lovers of enlightenment in our nation admit that if there has ever been an example of bravery and honesty in the whole province of Irevan up to the present, it was Muhammadgulu bey. If I say that the late Muhammadgulu bey did as much for his nation as the French revolutionaries did for their own, it will not be enough. I confess that other nations have erected monuments to such men,

---
[*] *Shua* - sun beam.

they are preserved as gifts, passing from time to time, from century to century. Unfortunately, a monument has not been erected to this martyr of the nation who was a rare creation, with innate talent.[21] This being so, I am happy to write the tragic biography of this great man and present it to the nation and to my compatriots as an example of great misfortune.

Biography, or the Date of his Death

The late Muhammadgulu bey was born in 1864 in the town of Nakhchivan. His father was Major Shafi aga, one of Nakhchivan's noblemen. He received his initial and most important education, more exactly, his initial upbringing and training, from his father. His second education, that is, his primary education, came from private teachers.

He was first brought up at home, which is a natural school and, when old enough to continue his education abroad, he entered the military school in Tiflis, as had his father before him. Then he continued his education in Petersburg in the Mikhailovsky Higher Military School of Artillery. In 1882, he achieved the rank of non-commissioned officer. In 1884 he graduated from the school of artillery with the rank of officer.

For a good length of time he served the nation, the state and his motherland as an officer. With his divine talent and the dignity of a man he won the respect of all. By his skill and ability he rose to the rank of captain, never sparing his life in the service of the nation and motherland. He served in the army until 1893. After serving the state and motherland with sword and banner, he decided to test himself in the art of penmanship.

He retired with the rank of junior-captain and returned home. He stayed in his motherland, in his birthplace - Nakhchivan - for

---

[21] An item of sculpture or architecture erected in memory of a great man, or of a great event, for future generations is called a monument. The word monument (abida) was first used in this sense by Haji Efendi, a teacher, and it is accepted by everybody. May God bless his pure soul!

one or two years, then he went to the town of Irevan. He observed the life of his nation, which he loved more than his own life, and began to study its needs. He learned that all the Muslims in the province of Irevan suffered because of their lack of knowledge, science and education. They did not know foreign languages - Russian, first of all - their own rights, the laws of the country or the duties of local and higher officials. He understood that the Muslims needed a lawyer, a good advocate, to defend their rights, and it was necessary to start from that point. By using all his knowledge, courage, desire and strength, he began to prepare for examinations to become a lawyer. He soon got his diploma. He became a skilful lawyer, with a profound knowledge of the law - as he had previously become a good artillery officer. He joined the might of his sword to that of his pen. By his perfectionism and courage, devotion and nobility he soon won great popularity. People who had appealed to the services of prominent Petersburg lawyers began to make use of his eloquent and logical speech and legal knowledge. His work, convincing speech and his promise always produced immediate and positive results. This great martyr of the nation managed to resolve difficult and complicated cases successfully - much better than the famous, experienced lawyers of Irevan. His dignity and skill, in combination with his nobility, love for the nation and compassion, engraved his name on everybody's heart. Like many lawyers, he was not lured by money or property. He demonstrated his nobility physically, spiritually and morally. He was generous, never disclosed a desire for wealth, his aims were noble and he had a broad world outlook. His speech was logical, he possessed high intellect and his courage and thinking, efforts and persistence, his love for the nation and his devotion were all praiseworthy. Many poor, miserable Muslims came to his house every day, told him of their complaints and he put them down on paper. He did this like a doctor giving medicine to his patients free of charge. He was always busy, nevertheless, he took part in all events in his community, and he was the central figure in them. There was not a day when he did not do something for the benefit of his people. Thus this martyr of the nation, who lived for the highest goals, never forgot the education and upbringing of the nation's children, even though he was busy with affairs of great importance. He thought about the health and progress of the nation. According to him, the priority for the nation was to inaugurate schools to meet the demands of the time. Despite his work as a lawyer, which was very hard and took up much time, he opened a boarding school named *Leyli** for Muslim girls, the first in the Caucasus. First a retired officer, then a lawyer, now he began to function as an educator. He became an educational example, a teacher of teachers who spent their lives teaching but could not open boarding schools for Muslims in many large towns in the Caucasus. Within a brief period his boarding school became one of the most highly developed. He spent most of his time either at school or in his office, working as a lawyer. Finally, he went to Petersburg as a lawyer, to defend the Muslims of Irevan in March of that year.

This great and important task demanded courage and a profound knowledge of the law. Thus it was decided to lay the responsibility on Muhammadgulu bey. The task required a man able to fulfil this subtle and very important work. The residents of Irevan did not have any difficulty in finding such a man, because there was Muhammadgulu bey, who was as unshakable as a mountain, as brave as a lion, as intelligent as Khizr (one of the Muslim prophets) able to unravel every mystery and as industrious as an ant. Poor man... He set out for Petersburg with several men chosen and supported unanimously by the residents.

He delivered the needs and complaints of the residents to the Viceroy, Count Vorontsov, and to the Minister of the Interior. Being responsible for defending the rights of the poor nation in government institutions, he used his tongue and pen skilfully. His goal was to achieve equal rights for the Muslims, alongside other nations, including the Armenians. This request by Muhammadgulu bey offended the latter, who considered themselves to be superior to the

---

* Leyli, i.e. a night school, a kind of boarding school.

other nations in the Caucasus. They began to send him letters, threatening to make him shahid.[*]

They were waiting for his return from Petersburg, to kill him by any means. Muhammadgulu bey was aware of their intention. But he was not afraid that some cowardly Armenians would fire at him from behind a wall. He wanted to continue his work at the school and in his office as a lawyer. But nobody helped him in this work. Disappointed and desparate, he gave up the school and his work as a lawyer, and decided to go to Paris and serve his nation from there.

This lover of his nation, this example of bravery, wanted to take his nephew Heydar and others to Paris and open the door to education and upbringing for Caucasians. He wanted to mediate in the arrival of Caucasians in Paris for education, to help them learn about the capital of France, and to be a source of knowledge and courage. With these thoughts in mind he left Irevan for Tiflis on 25 August. He completed his work there and, together with his nephew Heydar aga, left for Batumi in order to sail to Paris. He bought tickets for the ship and waited for its departure. There was still an hour to wait. To make use of the time he began to write letters to his friends, "We are in Batumi, have our tickets. In an hour we shall board a French liner and leave for Paris. I shall never forget my nation, my motherland. Service to the nation does not depend on time and space, it depends on man's own self..." He dropped his last letter into the letter box and decided to go for a meal. At that moment three callous Armenians appeared from behind the wall where they had hidden themselves, stabbed and cut this lover of the nation to pieces with their daggers and then escaped. The province of Irevan had, perhaps, never brought up such a brave man. The whole Caucasus could be proud of him, he was the apple of the eye of the nation, he was knifed at the age 41 by a few traitors and cowards.

This sacred, dagger-wounded body, which will surely rest in paradise, remained in Batumi for two days, then, with the help of

---

[*] Martyr, deceased, fallen for a just cause.

the Muslims of Batumi, the consul of Iran and other noblemen, it was sent to Tiflis, accompanied by his nephew Heydar[22]

The residents of Tiflis met the body with great tribute and solemnity at the station. He was taken first to the mosque, washed and then buried in the cemetery next to his sister. The late Muhammadgulu bey was a pure and honest Muslim. Stabbed by a dagger, he uttered his last words. Let everybody know this. After receiving blows to his head he fell and then got back to his feet, leaned against the wall and said: "There is no God but Allah and Muhammad is His messenger. There is no God but Allah, be my witness that I always served my dear nation." When the murderers heard these words, they stabbed him in the heart and he fell to the ground. May God endow his nephew, his brother and all other Muslims with courage and mercy!

---

[22] Heydar aga, nephew of the deceased Muhammadgulu bey, whom he was to accompany to Paris, is a man of common sense. I have met him personally. He is very clever and kind-hearted. I introduce him to readers in memory of his uncle.

The Empty Illusions of the Armenians of Javanshir

As we know, the Armenians dreamed of driving the Muslims from the province of Ganja and establishing their own state there. What has been written about the events in Javanshir above and below is sufficient proof of their dreams. Further proof is in their destruction of all the Muslim villages in the Terter Gorge and yet more evidence is the destruction of Muslim villages in the Khachin Gorge. The Armenians dreamed of destroying these villages and laying a highway from Ganja to Shusha; this was the task of the Armenian Committee. The committee had allotted 60,000 manats for the purpose. The road was to be laid by early March and would cross the village of Kolanli. The construction of the highway fell in the period when Governor General Goloshapov assisted the Armenians to destroy Shusha. Following complaints from the Muslims, he was substituted by General Bauver and the construction of the highway was forbidden. The residents of Kolanli were sent back to their village by order of General Bauver and under his protection, because the villagers lingered and did not know where to go. The remnants of the road can still be seen in Kolanli. The Armenians tried hard to achieve their goal in the district of Javanshir, bribing all the officials responsible and also destroying many Muslim villages. Finally, on 1 January 1906, they were defeated in the battle of Papravend and left as many trophies and equipment on the battlefield as they had previously taken away. Their dreams collapsed completely, together with their policy in Shusha and in other districts.

The events in Javanshir

Here we shall speak about the events which suddenly erupted in the district of Javanshir of the province of Ganja from 1905-1906.

We first received information about the tragedies there through the newspaper *Irshad*. Here is a letter by Bakhish bey Yusifbeyov, published in a magazine in Russian. We have translated and adapted it to the understanding of our readers. The letter contains criticism, as well as positive ideas.

Introductory information about the administration of the district and its privileged residents

The district of Javanshir is divided into three areas, each having its own police station.

In the first and second areas all the villages belonged to the Muslims except Hasangaya, Serv, Yarimja, Sistula and Kakhlilar. The two areas are interconnected and subordinate to each other. The residents of these villages are very reputable, mighty and are Muslims. As the Muslims formed the majority in these two areas, there were no troubles, battles or crimes. The Muslims, being kind in nature, did not offend their humble Armenian neighbours. They treated their neighbours with ever-increasing love and did not commit any misdeeds to stain the pages of the nation's history.

The third area consisted of mountainous villages, the residents of which were mainly wealthy Armenians. The Muslim villages in this area were Demirli, Hajigarvend, Chiragli, Umudlu, Imaret Garvand and the villages along the River Khachin, namely Shakhavend, Konapay, Aliagali, Sirkhavend, Ismayilbeyli and others. They were all in the mountains and, taken together, the group of villages was called Kolanlar.

The majority of Armenians were trying to capture these villages. If their goals are studied, it becomes clear that they were looking for a road to enable the Armenians of Irevan, Shusha, Zengezur and Ganja to communicate with each other. That is, they wanted an Armenian soldier with his rifle on his shoulder from Irevan or Shusha to be able to go to any place he wanted without having to take a turn, that is, straight; if one looks at the geographical location of the Muslim villages, it is clear that they present serious obstacles to the Armenians' road. Thus the Armenians were making all kinds of preparations to attack these poor villages. Members of the Dashnaksutyun Party were resorting to different stratagems to direct their wrath against these Muslim villages, with the aim of destroying them.

Their goal was to slaughter all the Muslims in the two gorges and organize their Armenia there. Had these villages been destroyed, then the three districts mentioned above would have fallen under Armenian rule. With this in mind, the Armenians began to ill-treat their Muslim neighbours.

Whenever they had a chance, they took to looting and did things incompatible with humanity. The Muslims had been used to hearing "God Bless You" from the Armenians for many years, but now, when they heard swear words, insults, other offensive and injurious words, or when they witnessed the looting and murder committed by neighbours who had godfathered their sons and who had very often hosted them at night during their long travels, they were confused, and they could do nothing but complain to the government from time to time. In this way grief and feud ruled the two nations, and it brought them great misfortune and disaster. In those days the Armenians and Muslims had broken off all relations, the Armenian villages had actually become military headquarters and training grounds for members of the Dashnaksutyun.

Making use of the riots in Shusha and Karabagh in August 1905, the Armenians of the district of Javanshir began to act by and by; they began to insult, to scold, to discredit their Muslim neighbours whenever there was an opportunity. In this way they created a hatred of Armenians among the Muslims.

Armenian battle preparations

After completing their preparations for battle, the Armenians began to move the Armenian population of their villages in the first and second areas to the third area. All the villages except Serv are in this area. The third area was like a real battlefield. It was like the town of Magadan in Russia, the Salanik settlement in Turkey, Tokyo in Japan and Athens in Greece. It was a place filled with soldiers and weapons, ready for war.

After all these preparations the Armenians began to dig trenches and build fortifications in the Armenian villages close to Muslim ones. As with the fortifications built by mighty states, the trenches were dug in a special order and form. The Muslims did not take this seriously, looking upon them as a joke; they resembled fortifications used in children's games. According to the information at our disposal, the behaviour and actions of the Muslims can only be regretted; they arouse only amazement and pity. While the Armenians were buying fast repeater rifles, the Muslims were even selling their old rifles, "Gara Mahmud", made in Lahij* and handed down from their forefathers, to the Armenians for a suitable price. If I call these Muslims strange creatures, I will not be much mistaken. Seeing such shameful actions by the Muslims of Javanshir, the Armenians openly tried to acquire more firearms (Why they bear the name of Javanshir I do not know)

News of the riots

On 26 September 1905, a group of Dashnaksutyun members, engaged in the transportation of firearms, brutally murdered a Muslim by the name of Asad. This made a big impression on the Muslims and they thought hard about pursuing the Armenians. On the same day the Muslims confiscated several sacks of powder, bombs and some rifles sent from Switzerland. The police officials arrived at the scene of the crime and took away the arms and ammunition listed below.

---

* Lahij - a village in Azerbaijan, famous for its artisans producing copperware and weapons.

The investigation revealed that two boxes filled with powder and bombs were to be delivered to teachers in the village named Andriyans, Mirzayans and Sabah Saakyans, instead of copy-books for their pupils. Besides this, three men surrendered by the Muslims to chief of police Mirza Zakharbeyov were arrested. Several days after the incident, old Hummet bey Pasha bey oglu, a man of sixty and a resident of the village of Hajigarvend, was taken captive by the Armenians. The police demanded his return many times, but their demands were ignored. The governor general knew that if the Armenians did not return the captive, a national movement of the Muslims would be inevitable. He sent a message to the Armenians saying that if they ignored his order, then he would be obliged to send punitive troops against them. Only then did the Armenians agree to return Hummet bey. Now let us see how he was returned! Unfortunately, a punitive troop consisting of 100 Cossacks returned the corpse of the poor captive, bleeding and having been hidden for several days. Around that time the brothers Abasgulu and Iman, sons of Hasan khan and residents of the village of Sirkhavend, were killed and then burnt by the Armenians as they were going to the forest for fire wood. Only their severed heads were left at the scene of the crime as a token for their poor father to see. The poor man took the severed heads home for their mother as a keepsake. In those days elections to the local administration in the Caucasus were being held, but several dishonest beys of the district of Javanshir, lacking any feelings of patriotism, did not allow this poor father to appear before the crowd to ask the people for help.

Ah! What is hidden in Javanshir* and in this family name? Although the patience and tolerance of the Muslims had been exhausted, their beys engaged in mirth and orgy, pigeon-fancying and hunting with falcons; they lulled the poor Muslims to their own interests and subjected them to the blows of the Armenians (We think that these beys are worse than the Armenians, or simply second Armenians). Albeit with great difficulty, the Muslims main-

---

* Javanshirs - A Turkic clan. Panahali bey, founder of the Karabagh Khanate was originally from this clan.

tained their tolerance, thinking that the government would find a remedy, but the government did nothing and severely disappointed them. News of looting and murders committed by Armenians in the village of Sirkhavend also upset them. When the news arrived, a troop of one hundred Cossacks and officers were sent to the village. They saw that the village had been destroyed and burnt and there were no residents there. This is what they learned.

The events in Sirkhavend

At dawn on 3 October 1905, the low sound of a trumpet came from the forest. It was followed by infantry troops and cavalry with banners who attacked the village. They approached, captured the significant heights and positions and then began firing at the village.

Startled by the sound of firing, the Muslims took their families and left for the forest. Four hundred mounted Armenians pursued them and many Muslims were murdered. These mounted Armenians, commanded by Hamazasp,[23] destroyed the village completely. Soon Muslim corpses were scattered about the streets, there were pools of blood. The neighbouring Muslim village of Aliagali soon shared the same fate. The estates of the landlords Ismayil bey and Javad aga Javanshir were also looted and burned. The brutes did not spare suckling babies; they burned them in their cradles, took them from their mothers' arms, struck them against walls and stabbed them with bayonets.

One can not imagine the effect these events had on the Muslims. One day later news of the tragic event reached the settlement of Terter. General Tagashvili invited the representatives of both nations in Terter for peace talks. The Muslims came in great numbers, but not a single Armenian appeared. The Muslims informed the governor-general about the looted villages. The governor general dispatched 300 Cossacks to search for the perpetrators. They could not capture any of Hamazasp's soldiers as they did not follow the direct

---

[23] Hamazasp had participated directly in a number of battles in Karabagh, committing unimaginable barbarities; for this the Dashnaksutyun Committee conferred the rank of general on him.

road to the village, but went through the trackless wilderness!? Of course, it was impossible to capture them, because all the Armenian villages had promised the Committee that they would conceal them. The Muslims were slightly relieved, they believed that the government would take some measures, thus they remained silent and did not take any action. The government again kept the poor Muslim villages under the oppression of the beys. The deceived Muslims living in the third area continued to be victims of Armenian brutality.

The Muslims of the district, who had lived in these conditions for over a month, complained to government officials from time to time, because crimes, although not very serious, were very frequent. Of course, we do not have the time or space to deal with all of them here. At this point Pivovarov was appointed chief of police of Shusha district and Fligbel, the previous chief of police, was dismissed.[24]

The events of 30 November 1905, or Pivovarov's working methods

At the end of November a well-known resident of the village of Hajigarvend, Gochag Askarkhan, was going to fetch his uncle's family from the summer pasture accompanied by twenty armed Muslims. The Armenians learned about this and organized an ambush by the bridge of Serseng in Terter.

Police Chief Pivovarov did nothing to investigate the Muslims' complaints and left them at the disposal of the savage Armenians. Peace was breached throughout the district of Javanshir, troubles and disorder raged everywhere. The roads were closed to peaceful travellers. The roads in Javanshir, along which merchants' caravans had

---

[24]Chief of police Pivovarov was a high-ranking government official and took part in many crimes. He supported the Armenians in Shusha and other places; because of this the Muslims were against his appointment to the district of Javanshir. Pivovarov was on friendly terms with the Armenian parties, displaying love and sincerity to the Dashnaks. The villagers and the merchants of Shusha appealed to the governor general to remove him from the post of chief of police, but in vain, because the dishonest beys (rich nobility) appealed to the same governor general to keep Pivovarov. This is it - the family name of Javanshir! And the governor-general kept Pivovarov in his post in order not to offend the beys.

once moved day and night, became as silent and lifeless as the desert.

Communications between the Muslim villages were broken, people lacked food, as they had not received anything from outside for three months; hunger and fear for their lives terrified the Muslims.

But the beys and landlords of Javanshir feasted and enjoyed their time with Pivovarov every day.

25 November 1905

The tragedy of Demirli on 27 November 1905

At dawn on 27 November, Dashnaksutyun troops, together with Armenian volunteers from the villages of Madagiz, Chayli, Namisa and others, surrounded the Muslim village of Demirli. Demirli was surrounded by Armenian villages on three sides, but neighboured the Muslim village of Chiragli to the west. The Armenians attacked first on three sides and occupied significant positions. They first killed four shepherds and drove away their 1500 sheep to an Armenian village. Then they fired their repeater rifles at the village. There were at that point only four men in the village. These brave men occupied good positions and fought against 10,000 Armenians until the evening and protected the village. The rest of the residents took their families and moved towards the village of Chiragli and the wilderness.

The four men fought until dusk. When they ran short of cartridges they escaped and saved themselves. Then the Armenians looted whatever they saw and could take, then set fire to the houses.

The residents of Demirli exceeded other villages in the district in wealth and property. Most of the villagers had over 500 sheep. Saving only their lives, they found shelter in the village of Chiragli. The district chief of police went to Demirli with one hundred Cossacks and found the village in flames. Of two thousand sheep he could find only five hundred; he returned them to their owners.

In this battle the Muslims lost eight men killed, the Armenians lost about forty. The Muslims complained to the police chief, named the looters from the Armenian villages and identified for him the sheep, cattle and other property, but he did not trouble himself and ignored their complaints. The plaintiffs regarded the behaviour of the chief of police as that of an accomplice to the criminals. If everything is examined in detail, however, then we shall see that justice was on the side of the police.

The Armenians would otherwise not have allowed the police to be fair and just in the investigation of their crimes for a single moment. The gluttonous and voracious police were bribed by the Armenians; thus they ignored the complaints and cries of the Muslims and did not even want to listen to them. As for the Muslims themselves, they committed no atrocities and made no military preparations to fight the Armenians. Unlike the latter, they did not have sufficient money to satiate the police, the chiefs and the nobility.

Instead of terror groups, the Muslims had poor communities; instead of modern arms and modern rifles, they had old muskets; instead of money they had bleeding livers, as a result of the negligence of the government officials; instead of brave and honest chiefs they had dishonest, shameless, satanic landlords and beys. Thus the Muslims were oppressed from all sides, they were all obliged to take their families and move from one village to another. In each village they encountered sad tales that made them sigh. The murder of the residents of Kolanli and the complete destruction of the village angered and disappointed them.

The Muslims attempted several times to set up a council to discuss these issues, but because of the negative stance of the beys, the idea did not become reality.

The needs of the Muslims of Javanshir to be raised in the council - or fruitless initiatives

After witnessing the ubiquitous aggression of the Armenians, and being completely unarmed, the Muslims finally set up a council to discuss the following items:

1. The Muslims should purchase repeater rifles and other weapons.

2. The Muslims should not remain on the defensive, but must attack and drive the Armenians out.

3. If war is waged against Muslims anywhere, they must go to help the fighters with all means, including equipment.

Destruction of the council by the beys, or news of the events in Chiragli and Hajigarvend on 31 November 1905

When the beys of Javanshir became aware of the council of Muslims, they began to threaten its founders and would not allow them to unite and fight against the Armenians. At this very moment, tragic events took place in the villages of Hajigarvend and Chiragli on 31 November.

As mentioned above, these two villages are very close to each other. All the armed residents had gone to bring back the family and cattle of Askar khan's uncle from the summer pastures. Taking advantage, the Armenians, with a troop of volunteers and Dashnaksutyun soldiers, surrounded the village at dawn on 31 November, and fired at it from all sides. The unarmed residents were not able to resist; after some skirmishing they took their families and withdrew to the village of Purkhud. The Muslims lost 10 persons killed, the number of Armenians killed in the battle was about one hundred. When news of the slaughter and looting in the villages of Chiragli and Hajigarvend reached administration areas 1 and 2, a detachment of 200 mounted Muslim militants hurried to help. On their way they destroyed the Armenian village of Chayli and set about 100 houses on fire, but could not return the looted property of the Muslims, because the Armenian militants had already disappeared.

Note: For the attention of our distinguished reporter Mr. Yusifbeyov!

Mr. Yusifbeyov! I have added some other information from different sources to that which you sent us about the tragedies in Javanshir. Here again I think that I have the right to add something to your information, for which I beg your pardon.

My dear sir, by praising your beys of Javanshir a little, do you want to make the people aware of their decent treatment and behaviour?

My dear sir! In those parts of the Caucasus where the Armenian-Muslim tragedies took place, the chiefs and officials of the local authorities have been completely coldblooded and have betrayed both of the nations more than once. There have also been brave, honest and fair men. Alongside them, we have always witnessed the victory of the treacherous and the cowards. And it is clear from your letter that the beys of Javanshir have been most treacherous and dishonest.

Do not trouble yourself too much to praise them! Some of the Javanshir beys reside in Zengezur. They have also disappointed the nation greatly. I appealed to them several times through the newspaper *Irshad*, but did not get an answer worthy of them. I do not think that in the province of Ganja there has remained anyone honest enough to bear the family name of Javanshir except the late Ahmed bey Javanshir.* Do not be offended, my brother!

The latest situation in the villages of Hajigarvend and Chiragli

After the destruction of these two villages, chief of police Pivovarov became aware of it and ordered his assistant to take five Cossacks with him and go there and, if the complaints of the Muslims were true, to resolve them. His assistant Smorodsky, who was a bitter enemy of the Muslims, saying "it is impossible to go there with just five Cossacks, it is very dangerous," returned after not even getting half way. This was the help rendered to the Muslims by the police. This is how they treat the Muslims. Know this, Muslims!?

---

* Ahmed bey Javanshir (1828-1903), historian. The author of a book on the political history of the Karabakh Khanate (1747-1805)

In short, the villages of Chiragli and Hajigarvend were burned to ashes. The residents first assembled in the village of Purkhud, then, thinking that it had also been surrounded by the Armenians, they left and moved to other Muslim villages in administration area 2. The Armenians looted and burned that village, too. It is evident from the information obtained that, from 3 October to December, the Muslim villages of Demirli, Chiragli, Hajigarvend and Purkhud were burned and turned to ashes.

In the Terter Gorge only the Muslim village of Umudlu remained untouched. This village was also surrounded by Armenian villages on all four sides. It was located 40 versts from the part of the district populated mostly by Muslims.

Everybody must know that the tragedy of the village of Umudlu was the most painful and heartrending of all. No nation or people has ever been subjected to so much trouble and torture as that committed by the Armenians. You will not find in any history so much oppression committed by man against his own kind. The residents of Umudlu suffered greatly. Their property was looted and people killed. You can not find any village in the whole Caucasus which has suffered so much as Umudlu.

The miserable state of the village of Umudlu

When the residents of the village of Umudlu saw that the above-mentioned villages had been destroyed by the Armenians, they also decided to abandon the village. For this purpose they sent Ismayil, head of the local administration, to Terter, to the district chief of police, to ask him to ensure their security with several Cossacks when they left the village. Pivovarov, chief of police, refused to fulfil the request, giving various reasons. The head of the local administration said the following: "Hence it is impossible for the residents of Umudlu to remain in the village". The chief of police didn't say anything. Ismayil returned home in disappointment. The residents decided, after a long discussion, to leave the village and leave everything to the disposal and mercy of God.

The residents of Umudlu leave the village and are subjected to slaughter

After losing hope that government troops would ensure their security, on the morning of 26 December 1905 they loaded their most precious possessions onto carts, took their families, flocks of sheep and cattle, and left the village. When passing the Armenian village of Heyvali, they met Aram bey Hasan Jalalov,[25] representative of the local administration in the village. The latter asked them not to walk in the dark of the night but to spend the rest of the night in the village and set out at dawn. He said that it was a shame for them to move at night. The poor, naive Ismayil was deceived by the sweet, satanic words of the Armenian and advised his villagers to spend the night in Heyvali. They stopped the carts and let the animals and the people rest. The night was cold and they made a fire to warm themselves. Then the villagers heard the sound of a trumpet. It was a detachment of Dashnaksutyun members in ambush. Although everybody heard the trumpet, no one thought anything of it, particularly Ismayil. He was sure that Aram bey would not harm them because he had done him many good turns in the past. At this moment the Dashnaks surrounded the poor Muslims and fired at them.

The unarmed Muslims did not know what to do. There was confusion. The Armenians separated the men from the women and cut the throats of the men like sheep. Leaving some of the women safe, they killed the rest.

In the confusion only 30 people found refuge from this human slaughterhouse. These facts were related by them. The Armenians tore the wombs of pregnant women, the heads of innocent infants emerged from them covered in blood. The women and girls scattered in all directions. Those who escaped said that several women were still being held as captives.

---

[25] Aram bey Hasan Jalilov was the head of the local administration of the Armenian village of Ranik. In the battle for Shusha, Ismayil helped him with food, sugar, lighting oil and other necessities of life. He believed that Aram would never commit such treachery and drown the residents of Umudlu in a pool of blood. Such is the fate of anyone, anywhere, who does good to others.

Note: I read the letter about the events in Javanshir sent by our distinguished reporter, but I could not read his words in full, because some lines were darkened and blotted by water. Therefore I have described the tragedy very briefly.

I think that not water, but the reporter's tears had dropped on those lines, because he could not write about the humiliated, insulted young and old women without shedding tears. He wrote the lines as he wept. I also read them with tears in my eyes, but did not want my readers to do the same.

My conclusion

If we look at the history of mankind, we shall see that up to now no nation has tortured women so much as the Armenians did the women of the village of Umudlu. They slaughtered children in the presence of their mothers. While the children were floundering in their death agony, the Armenians were raping the mothers, whose eyes were full of tears. What can be said about such men, or such a nation?

Is this Armenian culture?!! What will be the end of a nation with such satanic treatment, behaviour and desire for independence, I wonder? Can we say a nation is civilised if its representatives slaughter about 150 men and women, lay them in a pile and set fire to them?

As I have written above, our history has been unbiased, neutral; I maintain that same position. But when one sees such savagery by the Armenians, one's pen and feelings cannot remain unbiased.

If the tragedies of Javanshir had been properly committed to paper, then this would have been sufficient evidence of all the tragedies suffered by the Muslims. Being always devoted to peace, we have not written about a number of the tragedies committed by the Armenians, we have left them unpenned.

But we do want to mention one thing: that the beys of Javanshir and the police chiefs always helped the Armenians to put their plans into operation.

As a tragic scar across the heart of the nation, our history will never hide it. It will be written, made history and left to the future, as a memory of the motherland, nation, and also as a memorial to the tragedies suffered. I believe that it will be left for the future as I describe it.

In those years the Armenians moved their fellows from the villages of Hasangaya, Yarimja and Sistula to administration area 3.

Had the beys been honest, brave and lovers of their nation in those days and moved the Muslims to villages populated by Muslims, such tragedies would not have taken place at all. None of the honest, courageous beys, with the blood of a Muslim running in his veins, asked Pivovarov to move the Muslims of Umudlu to some other place under the protection of troops; had they done so, the poor Muslims would not have suffered such losses. No such man was found. Had the beys, who liked to mount horses and go hunting with falcons, been brave enough and lovers of the nation, the newly married women and 12-year old girls would not have been brutally raped by the Armenians and kept in captivity. My Prophet, raise your head from the grave!!!.... Raise your head and see how many indecent, dishonest and inhuman men bear the name of your subjects, who are completely unaware of Islam, who have acted with such dishonesty and disgrace.

The consequences of the events

The villages destroyed by the Armenians simultaneously with the village of Umudlu were the following: Umudlu and small settlements forming the village of Imaret Garvand. According to the information at our disposal, apart from those who were killed in the village of Umudlu, there were no human losses in these villages, but there was great material damage and loss of property. After the looting and destruction of these villages, the Armenians destroyed all the Muslim villages in the district of Terter, and then passed to the Khachin Gorge.

News of January. The beginning of 1906

In January, Armenian militants assembled and attacked the village of Shikhavend in the Khachin Gorge. After a skirmish lasting several hours they managed to drive the residents out of the village, then they looted it, set the mosque and its minaret on fire and fulfilled their national goal in these two gorges. Not satisfied with this, they continued their savagery. They then decided to attack the Daghbasar villages, to destroy them and, by and by, to march against the villages in the lowlands. The village of Papravend was a rich Muslim village. There were also enough young men able to fight the enemy. The village was very picturesque and located on the border of Armenian villages.

The battle of Papravend

The village of Papravend had sufficient young men able to wage a battle, therefore the Armenians did not treat it in the same way as other Muslim villages and, in order to attack it, they began to organize detachments of much greater size. After these preparation the Armenians, under the command of Hamazasp, attacked the village of Papravend on 1 January 1906. The battle raged the whole day. The Muslims bravely stood firm against the Dashnaksutyun volunteers. The battle continued till the evening. The Armenians were defeated and withdrew to the Armenian village of Agdere in disarray. When news of the Armenian attack on the village of Papravend reached the neighbouring Muslim villages, help came from all sides. The Muslims strengthened the village defences and organized effective reconnaissance. The Armenians also reinforced their forces and the next day they again attacked the village. The skirmishing was very fierce on that day. The Armenians fired their cannons several times. According to the evidence of an Armenian captive, on that day they fired 15,000 cartridges at the Muslims. The Armenians resorted to all the tricks of war but, as the Muslims demonstrated bravery and military prowess, they did not gain any advantage, suffered great losses of men and were obliged to withdraw. Muslim militants broke the front-line and began to pursue the retreating enemy. The Armenians dropped their weapons and tried to save their lives. They were so afraid of losing their lives that they even threw off their overcoats and coats to ease their burden. Among the things discarded the Muslims found a map of the battlefield, letters written by Hamazasp and journals dedicated to the problems of war. Further, the Armenians abandoned a cart full of cartridges, many daggers and repeater rifles on the battlefield. They also left their wounded behind; among them were soldiers not wounded, but dead from heart-attacks and fear. Many wounded soldiers lay under the hoofs of the horses of the Muslim militants who pursued the enemy. The Muslims murdered all the captured Armenian soldiers, to avenge the martyrs of the village of Umudlu. In this battle 120 Armenians were killed, the Muslims lost 15 men and about the same number were wounded. During the battle of Papravend the Muslims woke up a little and understood that they could not achieve anything by pleading with the Armenians, it was only necessary to take up arms against them.

Summary of events

In the district of Javanshir the Muslims were defeated, they suffered great losses of men and property. This was all because of the dishonesty and treachery of the beys and chief of police Pivovarov, who supported the Armenians, and also because most Muslims were unarmed. Again it must be repeated that all this happened because of the beys of Javanshir, who lacked decency and were devoid of love for the nation and motherland.

Correspondents' reports have not been altered

Painful Events in Ganja

Information about the events which began on 1 November 1905 was collected by Ali Akber bey Rafibeyov[*] from a magazine in Russian and from other letters. I have compiled and translated them. The Armenian-Muslim clashes took place in different parts of the Caucasus and, with the help of God, I received information about all of them. When they are analysed, the events in Ganja seem the most surprising of all. I learned everything. I also became acquainted with the arrogant collection of information in Russian assembled by Mr. Alibeyov,[**] who blamed the Muslims for the conflict. When I looked through the information collected by our distinguished correspondent, Akber bey Rafibeyov, and also through the reports of police chief Gamsaragan, an Armenian by nationality, dated 26 September 1905 (№ 8221) and his report 8048, it became clear that the Muslims had been in wretched condition and unaware of the riots. This is the opinion of the chief of police who was at the centre of all the events there. When we compare these two views, we see that there are many errors in Mr. Alibeyov's information.

Neither an honest Armenian nor Muslim can deny that members of the Dashnaksutyun Party were participants in and the instigators of many riots in Ganja. If this historical essay or my impartiality had allowed, I would have explained the Armenians' inhumane actions and made readers aware of them. I would also have liked to translate some lines from the information collected by

---

[*] Ali Akber bey Rafibeyov Kerbalai Hasan oglu (1839-1919), famous Azerbaijani socio-political figure. One of the organizers of Azerbaijani defence during the clashes, he wrote many reports on these events.

[**] See: I. Alibeyov. 'People's Verdict on the Bloody Days in Elizavetpol', Tiflis 1906.

Mr.Alibeyov to let people, and Mr.Alibeyov himself, know who was guilty of the troubles. But my conviction and faith do not allow me do any of this, and I am one of those who regret that such troubles took place.

The events in Ganja

At about 6 or 7 o'clock on 18 November 1905, when residents of the village of Tokhana in Ganja: Bayram Meshedi Mammadali oglu, Mehrali Zeynal oglu, Amrah Hasan oglu and Mirza Muhammadali oglu, were on their way home on the Kolanli road, an Armenian area, with horses laden with wheat, they encountered fierce fire from behind the Armenian gardens.

As a result, Bayram Muhammadali oglu and Mehrali Zeynal oglu were killed, the other two escaped and went to inform the police. When the shooting started, Amrah Hasanoglu abandoned his horse, with the wheat, by the bodies of the victims and ran off; the Armenians pursued, with the aim of killing him.

Thank God that several Armenian and Muslim coal dealers arrived on the spot at that moment; they rescued the poor man and returned his horse and wheat to him. At the same time, several coal dealers were walking from the town; they saw the dead Muslims lying in a pool of blood. They returned to the Mollajelilli quarter and spoke of the tragedy, asking people to take carts to fetch the bodies. When the residents of Mollajelilli heard the news, a group of Muslims headed by Salman Mehdi oglu and Karbalayi Muhammad Ibrahim oglu set out to collect the corpses. When they approached the spot, they saw the chief of police, Gamasaragan, his deputy Abil bey Gapanlinsky, town interrogator Ley Ogter and several policemen at the scene of the crime.

When comrades of the dead were interrogated, it became clear that the crime had been committed by Avetis Avetisov, Grigor Tiyunov and their friends. After recording the necessary details, they returned to the town in their phaetons. As for the Muslim residents of Mollajelilli, Abil bey Gapanlinsky advised them to avoid the direct road in order not to encounter the Armenians, and to walk through the gardens. But the Armenians fired at them fiercely in an ambush; they fired from the garden of Yerivant Yegayev. The Muslims were obliged to change direction in order to avoid the shooting. The shootings echoed through the town terribly. About one hundred armed Dashnaks emerged from the gardens. They occupied positions in groups of five or six, and continued to fire at the Muslims. The residents of Mollajelilli assembled and set out to rescue their brothers as soon as they heard the news. But they were obliged to return home, because the Armenians were fighting under the command of well trained army officers, while the Muslims were unarmed and untrained.

Chief of district police Gamsaragan was finally obliged to appeal to chief of the town police Hasan bey when he saw that the situation had deteriorated badly. In his turn Hasan bey sent detailed information about the events to Governor General Tagashvili. The General sent fifty Cossacks under Orlov's command and ordered him to suppress the trouble. When the Cossacks approached the scene, they were fired on by the Armenians from positions occupied in advance. According to Mohsun, a Muslim policeman, police chief Gamasaragan sent Ter-Yapramov and other Armenians to the town's first quarter to assemble all the Armenians there and tell them about the clashes in the second quarter. The Armenians of the first quarter closed their shops and marched towards the second quarter.....

Then the Armenians sent by Gamasaragan spread rumours and fired several pistol shots in front of Haji Muhammad Huseyn Rafiyev's shop and in this way incited the Muslims to fight.

We got this information from Karbalayi Ali Baltachi oglu and other well-known residents of the town. It is further proof of the truth of the information below, that the Armenians had hidden arms in their shops and made preparations in advance. It became clear from the report of chief of police Gamasaragan about the event, dated 26 November 1905 (№ 8221), and from the evidence of residents of Mollajelilli, as well as from Orlov, commander of the Cossacks, deputy police chief Abil bey, members of the office of the governor and officials in charge of imperial property that the fighting was begun by the Armenians at about 9 o'clock in the morning and only met a Muslim response at 10.45. It also became clear that, until that time, the Muslims sat in peace, waiting. There was not much skirmishing in the first part of the town, because the Armenians rushed into the second part, continuing that skirmish.[26] While they made preparations to rush to the second part of the town, the Muslims sat quietly, due to lack of arms and ammunition. Soon the sounds of gunfire echoed in all parts of the town, people of various nationalities assembled in the bazaar. The crowd was so big that one could not estimate its number. This was all to the good: first there were peasants who had mostly come to sell food products. Then there were Georgians, who had changed their clothes to avoid confusion, and also Iranians, Lezghins, and soldiers of many nations.

When this multi-hued crowd began to loot the shops there, they did not care whether the shop belonged to a Muslim or an Armenian. Apart from the Russian women and civil workers, everybody was taking part in the looting and murder, and setting fire to houses and shops. On 19, 20 and 21 November, there were odd shootings, but nobody was injured. On those days the deputy governor, General Malama, made attempts to restore peace temporarily and the Armenians promised to cease firing.

News of November 23

Although the Armenians had promised General Malama that they would cease firing and skirmishing, on the night of 23 November they again unexpectedly and treacherously attacked the Muslims.

With their base ambition, they sent scouts to learn what the Muslims, who were living peacefully, were doing and whether they were making any war preparations.

---

[26] Our distinguished reporter does not say why the Armenians left the market in haste, but the letters we have received give this account. When the Armenians retreated they were so afraid of losing their lives that the retreat became a rout.

Armenian scouts, consisting of 12 men, crossed the River Ganja, and hid in the mill of Tagi Agahuseyn oglu, a resident of Ganja. The Armenian detachments remained on the other bank of the river, ready to attack and waiting for information from their scouts.

Thank God that the Muslims became aware of the Armenians' intentions in time and their defence detachments were waiting for the Armenians to pass through a narrow path. When the Armenians entered the mill, the Muslims' defence detachments occupied favourable positions and subjected them to fierce fire. The Armenians replied from several rifles. Then the Muslims left the ambush and attacked the Armenians, who threw themselves into the water in confusion and crossed to the other bank of the river. Then a bloody skirmish took place between the two sides. This continued from 3 o'clock at night until dawn. Had the sounds of firing and exploding bombs not been heard, it would have been imagined that red rain was falling from the heavens. Both sides expected to have many losses but, fortunately, the losses of the Armenians were greater, because their detachments had begun the attack in scattered formation. The situation was so grave that no fighter, be he Armenian or Muslim, could find time to dare to look up, or help anyone close to him, because of the sound of bullets. All found solace in the rifle pressed to their chests.

News of 24 November, or lasting peace

After the intense skirmishing of 23 November, deputy governor General Malama, a very kind and generous person, invited representatives of both parties to peace negotiations on the bridge which divided the town in two. On 24 November, people assembled on the bridge and began to wait for the peace negotiations. First the Sheikh-ul-Islam made an impressive speech, and then the floor was given to the Armenian Archimandrite, who delivered a speech calling people to peace. But his speech was not as impressive as the first one and it contained some false notes. Then the honourable residents of the town spoke of peace and its terms:

1. To exchange the captives taken in the fighting between November 18 and 24;

2. The election of representatives for the exchange of captives.

The representatives were chosen and sent to conduct the exchange. The first group of representatives included Andriyans Serebrakov with three Muslims, the second group included Verdiyev Abbas Huseyn oglu and Ali Alinagi oglu, the third group - Haji Molla Najafguluzade, Meshedi Rzagulu Zeynal oglu and Safar Muhammad Mustafa oglu, a Lezghin by nationality.

The representatives who went to get the captives and Armenian bodies from the Muslim quarter included:

the first group - Haji Samad Gojayev and Abil bey Gapanlinsky, with five Armenians - Atans and others

the second group - the chief of police and his deputy, Hasan bey Fatalibeyov, and three Armenians.

In short, when the representatives left to execute their duties, the crowd which had assembled to witness the peace negotiations also went home. Nevertheless, Hasan bey Fatalibeyov, who went to take the Armenian bodies from the mill of Haji Agahuseyn oglu, was fired at by the Armenians. The Armenians did it under the pretext that the Muslims were hiding the bodies. All the Muslim representatives executing the exchange of captives and bodies were fired at and bombed by the Armenians.

It became clear that either the Armenians were unaware of the peace achieved, or they were aware, but did not want to obey it. They killed three Muslim representatives of the peace-makers in Verdiyev's group. Their phaeton driver, Muhammadali Mirza oglu, saved himself by escaping from the scene. As soon as this news reached the Muslim quarters, the Armenian peace-makers, as well as the Armenians coming from the railway station, were attacked. In these fights eight Muslims, including Haji Molla Najafguluzade, a member of the governor's council, were killed (may they rest in peace). Only the Muslims in Serebrakov's group remained safe and sound. About the same numbers of Armenians were killed in the Muslim quarter. Two bombs were found by the bodies of the

Armenians scattered about the scene of the crime and they were given to deputy governor General Malama.

Peace breached, or the Armenians' answer

After this breach of the peace, the Armenians vehemently blamed the government representatives and the Muslims. Some of them said: "We had not yet informed the Armenians of the news, which is why the crimes were committed". Another group explained the breach like this:

"The peace agreement had been achieved by members of the Gnchak Party, therefore the Dashnaksutyun Committee tried to break it."

The Muslims were compelled to believe these words. Government officials were again making preparations for another peace agreement, whether they believed these words or not.

After all the above events, neutral government representatives arranged several peace assemblies, but the Armenians attended them unwillingly. Finally, they refused absolutely to take part. The Muslims, however, were for peace and armistice throughout, and did their best to achieve both.

The peace assembly was chaired by Mikhailov, a member of the governor's Council, and the exchange of captives was finally resolved. Again two groups were organized for the exchange of captives. One of the groups included Justice of the Peace Chernits and the above-mentioned Mikhailov; the other group consisted of Ali Akber bey Rafibeyov and Ali Asker Khasmammadov. The first group managed to exchange an Armenian by the name of Andriyans for three Muslims and by the efforts of the second group, an Armenian named Khojayev was returned. The Georgians taken captive by the Muslims had been released in advance. They were all held for taking part in looting.

An Armenian woman taken captive and held under protection was returned to the Armenians, but they refused to accept her for several reasons. But most of the Muslims taken captive by the

Armenians had been murdered either before the achievement of peace, or after it.

Summary of the correspondent's report

New peace agreement, new governor general

Fleisher, the new Governor General of Ganja, learned that the Armenians were not sympathetic to the peace achieved previously, therefore he ordered the organization of a new peace commission. Following the issue of the order a group was established. It consisted of 12 officers and 24 representatives - 12 Armenians and 12 Muslims. This group, chaired by Colonel Isayevich, began to work on a peace agreement.

Terms of peace

If the representatives of one party were unable to solve a problem, or acted in bad faith, resolution was the responsibility of the said 12 military officers. Many other terms were included in the peace agreement. The organization and work of this miscellaneous commission somehow restored peace and order to the town. But, later, the members of the commission made errors in the execution of their duties and the representatives of the parties seemed not to be disciplined or honest in their work; the residents of the town were left to work out their own destinies. To improve the situation in Ganja and throughout the province, the government was trying to strengthen its position by appointing new governors general distinguished by their valour and bravery. General Alftan was appointed Governor General of the whole province; General Levitsky - to the district of Gazakh; General Goloshapov, who was himself a murderer - to the district of Shusha. To silence the belligerents, the generals drafted a number of effective measures and fulfilled them.

The proof, or improvement in the situation

It was noted above that the trouble was begun by the Armenians at 9 o'clock in the morning and it then penetrated the Muslim quarter of the town. We have written about this, citing a number of cases in several places, but the malevolent Armenians never ceased to claim that "the Muslims attacked us all of a sudden on 18 November". In response, our esteemed correspondent has also added the cases below, endeavouring to save his nation from the slanderous accusations of the Armenians with proof.

The Armenians said that if the Muslims had intended to commit slaughter in advance, not a single Armenian out of about three thousand residing along the road to the railway station would have remained alive. If the Armenians had desired to cross to the Armenian quarter, they would have been murdered by the brutal Dashnaks standing between the two quarters of the town and separating them from each other. I shall describe all the savagery committed against the Muslims of Ganja.

1. On 8 November, five Dashnaks murdered Abbas Hasan oglu, resident of the village of Bahmanli, in Derebagin's garden.

2. In the Armenian quarter called Gosha Chinar, the Muslims Amir Aslan Ali Pasha oglu, Jabbar Huseyn oglu, Rustam Ismayil oglu, Rza Jabrail oglu and other residents of the village of Mollajelilli met a hail of bullets and were murdered by the Armenians for no reason. The crime was committed by Avetis Oganesov, the hatter Grisha, Vaso Amospirov and others.

3. The Cossacks found a beheaded body with his hands tied behind his back. He had been murdered by the Armenians. General Malama was particularly informed about this. Then the body of a Muslim by the name of Meshedi Sadig was found; he had been cut into pieces by the Armenians.

4. On 12 November, the Armenians killed Karbalayi Faraj Hasan oglu, who had worked as a millman for the Armenian Amospirov. The crime was committed by the Dashnaks. Chief of police Gamsaragan, Armenian by nationality, included this in his

report (№ 8048) to the respective authorities.

5. On 16 November, in the upper part of the village of Azad, in Boyuk Koloniya Street, two men from the village of Zurnabad, one of them by the name of Gasim Boyukkishi oglu and another unnamed Muslim, a resident of the village of Bahmanli, were caught by Armenians who tied their hands and left them lying on their backs. Some hunters found and untied them, then the poor men fled home. The police were informed about the incident.

6. On 18 November, the Armenians murdered Bayram Meshedi Muhammadali oglu, resident of the village of Tokhana. It is clear that, so far, about 30 innocent and unarmed Muslims have been murdered by the Armenians; this has been written about in detail: copies of the document are in the district police office. The Muslims tolerated all the brutalities of the Armenians in the town, because they were sure that such acts of violence would finally produce their bitter fruit and the guilty would be punished. And nobody knew why the Armenians behaved like that. When one notes their storing of arms and ammunition and mobilization of soldiers, then it is obvious that they were making preparations for a riot against the government. As the Muslims had not made military preparations for a single day, how could they dream of slaughtering the Armenians?!

Can a man of common sense slander such poor Muslims who had not made any preparations for war or stored arms?! There is no need to write about the Armenians' goals, because the telegrams of the Governor General[*] of the district of Gazakh (General Levitsky) to the viceroy are ample evidence. We must also note that the newspaper *Kaspiy* wrote about Dashnak activities on 9 March. The text of the article is the same as the text of the telegrams signed by General Levitsky.

---

[*] Should be: chief of the district

Tragedies in Tiflis

According to information in the newspapers, the government and population knew that the Armenian parties were guilty of all the troubles and conflicts in all corners of the Caucasus, and that people were compelled to stream towards Tiflis.

The newspapers in Tiflis have written various articles about these people. Readers are aware of them.

Along with the publication of such information, there were also rumours within the population about the Armenian-Muslim clashes. The poor Muslims were very few in number and powerless in Tiflis and so they were confused and desperate. They were depressed in Tiflis in those days and life was very hard for them there. The Governor General of Tiflis considered the critical state of the Muslims and issued a statement on 25 October 1905, to the following effect: "There are rumours in the town that there will be heavy clashes between the Armenians and Muslims. It is my duty to inform you that I have taken the necessary measures to quell any clashes or riots. I have charged the police with ensuring the security of the population and of their property. 25 October 1905. Signed, Zhbilyay". Despite the issuing of such statements and announcements, the Armenians were spreading rumours everyday in the town and discouraging residents from continuing their business. Seeing the miserable state of their compatriots, the Muslim leaders finally assembled and issued the following appeal to the residents: "Groundless rumours are being spread in Tiflis that there will be clashes and fighting between the Muslims and the Armenians. Because of this, we issue this appeal and tell our Muslim and Armenian brothers not to believe such senseless stories and to uncover the disseminators of these slanders. The provocateurs are not content with the innocent blood of the Muslims and Armenians which has reddened the lands of our country, but want to ruin this beautiful and picturesque Tiflis, too. We hope that the Muslims and Armenians of Tiflis are not so barbarous as to shed blood in vain, to wage war against their neighbours or inflict injury on each other. It is obvious that such rumours are spread by scoundrels who loot people's property when the parties are involved in clashes.

2 November 1905

In short, they soothed and silenced the Muslims in this way and assured the Armenians of their honesty and kind-heartedness. Despite these efforts by the government and the Muslims, the Armenians assembled a good number of soldiers in Tiflis and, by devious methods, they incited the Muslims into clashes. In this way several insignificant incidents took place before 20 November, but, due to lack of time and our desire not to excite and grieve readers more, let a description of the events which took place on 20 November suffice.

The events of 20 November

At 9 o'clock in the evening of 20 November 1905, there was a skirmish in the Muslim quarter of the town. It continued for about an hour and a half. Both Muslims and Armenians suffered great losses in this skirmish, but there was no exact information about the losses. The skirmish took place in the Kharpukh and Alavar quarters. Skirmishes continued the next day. We shall describe them one by one, based on the information at our disposal.

The events of 21 November 1905

Again, on this day a skirmish took place between the Armenians and the Muslims and continued very fiercely. It was raging in quarters 6 and 7, sometimes in 5 and 8. The Armenians and Muslims fired at each other continuously with pistols and rifles. It continued until noon. The two sides did not advance on each other, but fired from behind shelters.

Nobody knew the reason for the skirmish or who had started it. At about 12 noon a group of militants attacked the gun-shops of Ter-Sarkisov located in Golovinskiy Avenue, in Kursininskaya and Nikolayevskaya streets, and looted all the arms and ammunition in them. Then government troops appeared on the scene and the skirmish ceased. Members of the commission for armistice and peace, the town's police chief, clerics from both nationalities and representatives of the intelligentsia came to Alavar and began to calm both parties. The Muslims complained that the Armenians had begun the skirmish, firing at Muslims from Alavar. The Armenians accused the Muslims of firing first.

There was broken glass on the ground and the walls on both sides of the street bore traces of bullets. At 3 o'clock in the afternoon the railway workers went on strike and organized a meeting for peace.

Details of the meeting

At 3 o'clock in the afternoon of 21November 1905, the railway workers went on strike. Headed by the Social-Democrat Party, they marched from Nakhalovka towards the Muslim quarter along Agchal Street, carrying white flags. Their aim was to reconcile the two nations. The crowd was stopped by Major-General Rilski near the Vorontsov monument. He asked them to think about the meeting and its consequences, and he recommended they broke up and went home. The crowd moved towards the office of the viceroy to assure the Viceroy of the Caucasus, Vorontsov-Daskov, of their good intentions. The viceroy received them and encouraged the goodwill participants of the public movement.

Then the crowd walked from Vorontsov Square towards Soldat Bazaar and the Armenian Bazaar, then to Sheytan Bazaar and Garpiz Square.

The crowd was headed by the Governor of Tiflis, Rausch von Traubenberg.[*] The crowd grew larger and larger. In Garpiz Square

---

[*] Pavel Aleksandrovich Rausch von Traubenberq, State Advisor of the Tiflis Province from 4 August 1905 to 22 September 1907.

popular residents of the town made speeches and called both parties to peace. Some of the speakers uttered the following: "The instigators of the riots are provocateurs who incite people to violate public order." The governor said the statements had no basis. And, finally, they reconciled the Armenians and the Muslims.

News of the riots

In the first days of the riots 12 bodies were taken to the morgue at Mikhailovsky Hospital. Two of them were Armenians - a woman and a man, the rest were Muslims. One of the corpses was not identified. Thirteen men underwent surgery, three of them were Armenians, five were Muslims and five Georgians. The names of persons undergoing treatment at Mikhailovsky Hospital were known, but it was advised not to disclose them to the public.

The events of 24 November 1905

On 24 November, the skirmishing started again and both sides suffered great losses. Those wounded in the skirmishing were taken to Mikhailovsky Hospital. There were 13 Armenians and 2 Muslims. A further 6 Armenians and Muslims wounded in the skirmish were taken to the military hospital. On 25 November, the bodies of Arshak Garapetov, his son Aziz and four other Armenians were brought to Mikhailovsky Hospital. In those days the grocery of Mirza Akhundov was looted.

The events of 29 November

Sarkis, the owner of a sausage factory sent two armed Armenians and had the sausage factory[27] of his Muslim neighbour set on fire. Patriotic Georgians in the quarter demanded that Sarkis rebuild the factory and return it to his Muslim neighbour in work-

---

[27] In those riots both parties tried hard to inflict as much material damage on the opposition as possible. What Sarkis did to his neighbour was an economic attack, not a national one. Such things have always been commonplace.

ing order, otherwise they would compel him to do it. In this way the riots in Tiflis ended. Although small incidents took place, we will not comment on them, believing that they were not very significant.

Summary of events, 1905

On 20 November there was an attempt to instigate clashes between Muslims and Armenians in Tiflis. We are not aware of the reason for the conflict, but Armenians streamed into Tiflis from all over the neighbourhood and wanted to demonstrate their strength to the Muslims, knowing that they had not made military preparations; nor had they enough fighting forces.

In these clashes several Armenian shops were looted. A Muslim sausage factory was burnt and a grocery looted. The clashes took place mainly in quarters 6 and 7 and sometimes in 8, and weakened the Armenians greatly. The fighting, which began on 20 November, continued until 29 November.

In these clashes 24 Armenians were killed and about the same number were wounded. The Muslims had 15 men killed and wounded. The Social-Democratic Party restored peace and the hostilities ended.

Armenian-Muslim Clashes in Gazakh

When one compares the neighbouring Armenian and Muslim villages in the district of Gazakh, it is easy to conclude that the Muslim villages are very poor and weak.

Knowing this and being aware of the misbehaviour of their Armenian neighbours, the inhabitants of small Muslim villages moved early to much stronger Muslim villages. The smaller villages included Sofulu, Chakhmagli and others. Seeing that they were abandoned and ownerless, the Armenian neighbours looted and set them on fire, capturing several of the peasants left to guard the villages and killing a few of them. When the Muslim villagers heard this painful news, they could not bear it any longer; they attacked the Armenian village of Pipis (also abandoned) and set it on fire.

22 January 1906 was the Gurban holiday* (in remembrance of Abraham's sacrifice). The residents of the Muslim village of Gizilhajili were slaughtering the sacrificial animals and were at their holiday prayers. Armed Armenian detachments attacked the village, subjected it to a hurricane of fire, killed two Muslims, took an old, disabled man and two under-age girls with their mother captive, looted the village and set it on fire. Taken by surprise, the Muslims could do nothing but find refuge in neighbouring Muslim villages. When this incident occurred, Israfil bey and Nuru bey were visiting the village of Demirchiler. When they heard the skirmishing, they rushed to help the Muslims with a group of armed men. The Armenians could not resist them and were compelled to leave in haste. The Armenians did not respect neighbourly relations, human or civil rights. Seeing and experiencing such behaviour, the Muslims revived a little; Muslim volunteers attacked the

---

* Religious Muslim holiday of sacrifice.

village of Askipara from all sides. They lost four men killed. The Armenians left 80 bodies and a good number of arms and ammunition on the battlefield and were compelled to retreat.

The mounted Muslims who led the battle in Askipara fought in the day time and by night they moved the residents of the small Muslim villages to larger villages. These small villages included Askipara, Ayrim, Farahli, Baganis and others. No other significant events took place in this month. A detachment of 30 Cossacks sent to suppress the aggressive Armenians of the village of Karvansara were not supplied with ammunition and were ordered to return. Nevertheless, a colonel with several Cossack detachments set out for Karvansara with the same purpose on 31 January.

At that time Armenian-Muslim fighting broke out in the province of Zeyam. The residents of the Armenian village of Chardagli attacked Muslim villages. They were met by the armed guards of the Muslim villages of Irmashli and Ayibli, and a real battle took place. Armed Muslim detachments from other villages reached the battlefield to assist. The Armenian detachments could not resist and took to their heels. One Muslim was killed in the battle; the Armenians drove away ten horses, but left 15 dead on the battlefield. Many villages in the district of Gazakh were destroyed and burnt. The most populous of them were the following 12 villages: Alibeyli, Hajjali, Kazimli, Kohnegishlag, Yaradullu, Hagbeli, Sofulu, Jafarli, Chakhmagli, Gizilhajili, Kheyrimli and Baganis Ayrim.

There were three battles in the district of Gazakh. One of them was in the village of Alibeyli. We do not have exact information at our disposal about the losses in this battle. The Muslims did not suffer any losses there. The Armenians killed two Cossacks who had come to suppress the riot. The second was in the village of Tatli. Here the battle continued the whole day and two Muslims were killed. The Armenians lost about 50 men in the battle. The third was in the village of Askipara. In this battle the Muslims lost four, the Armenians had about 80 men killed. After these three battles government forces took control of the Gazakh district and a kind of peace was established. On 5 February government forces conducted searches of shops and houses in Gazakh. The Cossacks and dragoons inflicted great damage on the Muslims - a house was searched by about 50 soldiers and they stole whatever they came across. They broke all the lamps, crockery and similar items in all the houses they entered. They confiscated all the arms and ammunition in the Muslim villages, leaving not even a knife in the house. But they did not touch Armenian guns and cannons in Gazakh and the surrounding areas.

I have information about the events in Gazakh, but as information about the instigators of these troubles has not been clearly verified, we decided to publish only this letter. While Armenian-Muslim conflicts and clashes took place elsewhere, the Muslims of Gazakh were always eager to live with their neighbours in peace and harmony. Outwardly the Armenians seemed to be for peace, but in reality they were preparing to fight; purchasing rifles and ammunition of all kinds.

Such behaviour made the Muslims think. The Armenians were transporting goods from their shops to the mountainous Armenian villages, to Dilijan and Karvansara, which they thought were strongly defended. On a hard day for the Muslims, Mesrop, an Armenian and chief of police of Shamsaddin, and several Armenians in Muslim attire, went to Gazakh, loaded their rifles and fired at Muslims who were approaching them. Naturally, the Muslims returned fire, and the skirmish continued for some time. Then Mesrop and his men ran away. In this way they laid the foundations for the feud in Gazakh. Thus, when the above-mentioned three battles took place, the Armenians lost many people killed and the Muslims lost property. The information at my disposal gives me reason to believe that the Muslims suffered mainly because they were unaware of ongoing processes and because they were not represented at local or high level in the administration of the country. Before these events, the chief of police of the village of Tatli, Arsen

Arsenov, an Armenian, and the cleric Kinigar went to the house of Karbalayi Novruz Muhammad oglu, a resident of the village of Yaradullu, and to the houses of other villagers, and spoke of peace and armistice in order to deceive the Muslims. They said: "If the fighting spreads all over the region, we must not begin in this valley". In this way they demonstrated a deceptive kindness and friendliness.

The Muslims believed their words and continued to live in peace and comfort. As evidence, when 600 mounted Muslim volunteers set out from Gazakh to destroy the Armenian military centre in the village of Tatli, the Muslims of nearby villages met them with the Holy Koran in their hands and asked them to have mercy on their Armenian neighbours. Four days later the Armenians went to the village and said: "We are letting you know, because we are friends. If you want to remain alive, leave these villages tonight". Following this, the residents of the small villages moved to bigger villages. The next day those Armenian "friends" attacked cart drivers from the village of Yaradullu, killing five of them and taking nine captive. They looted about nine carts of barley and wheat belonging to the Muslims and set the villages on fire. The most terrible of those battles was the battle of Garagoyunlu. Here about 300 Armenians were killed and they were unable to continue the battle. We must also add that if the Muslims had had sufficient arms and ammunition in these battles, the Armenians would have been remembered only for their defeats in Gazakh province.

The Armenians had all the advantages in Gazakh, that is, most government officials and police were Armenians. So that several times at the outset of battles, police constables sold their rifles, or simply took them home. One of them was Sevan Tumanov. He murdered 15 neighbours of Bashir, a resident of the village of Atali, and drove away 800 cattle. These police constables would then return to the office and continue their work.

Note: The Caucasian Muslims' ignorance of world affairs and the Armenians' desire for independence recalls the predicament of the Muslims of Crete[28] in 1898. The Muslim villages in the Caucasus are in the same situation as that of the villages of Zafski, Akhladina, Vuri, Nasiya and Balyupchi in Crete.

Oh, poor Muslims!

Summary of events

The troubles in the district of Gazakh began on 29 November 1905. The Muslims were unaware of the existing state of affairs, thus they suffered great damage and losses. The majority of the police and government officials in Gazakh were Armenians and the Muslims suffered from their injustice. Three great battles took place there.

1. The battle of Alibeyli

2. The battle of Tatli. This battle continued for a whole day. Two Muslims and 50 Armenians were killed. About the same numbers of people were wounded. Two Cossack guards were also killed by the Armenians.

3. The battle of Askipara. Four Muslims and 80 Armenian militants were killed. The same numbers of people were wounded. The Armenian losses were greater. The cause of these clashes was Mesrop, police chief of Shamsaddin, who asssisted the Armenians greatly. Ten large and well-populated villages in Gazakh were destroyed; the names of those villages have been recorded in the detail of investigative reports. Besides those villages, many others were also destroyed.

---

[28] **Crete** - Greek Island in the Eastern Mediterranean.

Peace Negotiations in Tiflis

On 20 February 1906, in Tiflis, in the Green Hall of the viceroy's office, through the efforts and mediation of the Viceroy of the Caucasus, Vorontsov-Dashkov, an Armenian-Muslim peace assembly took place. This chapter deals with this assembly.

The aim of the assembly

The government officials in charge of the assembly:

Viceroy of the Caucasus Vorontsov-Dashkov, the governors of Tiflis, Irevan and Ganja, the viceregal deputies, Sultan Geray of the Crimea, General Malama, General Shirnikin and office clerk Peterson.

Muslim representatives to the assembly:

From Baku - Ahmed bey Agayev, Karbalayi Israfil Hajiyev, Alimardan bey Topchubashov, from Tiflis - Muhammad aga Vekilov, Doctor Garabeyov, from Ganja - Aliakber bey Khasmamedov, Adil khan Ziyadkhanov and others.

Armenian representatives:

Kalantar, editor of the newspaper *Musak*, from Tiflis - Khatisov, Samson Arutyunov, from Baku - Khatisov, Musheksyan, Doctor Stepanov, Arakelyan, Tagiyanusov, Ter-Avanesov, Archimandrite Muradyan and others.

Statement of the aims

The Viceroy of the Caucasus issued a decree to convene a peace assembly on 15 February, but the representatives of the Armenian side arrived only on 20 February and so the assembly did not begin its work on time. At the time appointed by order of the viceroy, the Muslim and Armenian representatives went to the Palace of Paradise (Humayun). They assembled in the Green Hall. After waiting for a while, the viceroy solemnly entered the hall. After opening the assembly he addressed the participants with the following words: "Gentlemen! The Caucasus, your dear motherland, has already been subjected to these misfortunes for one year. The government has done a great deal, but no result has been achieved. We believe that these misfortunes must be removed for your own peace and security and for those of the Caucasus. The Armenian-Muslim riots are only of benefit to robbers and rioters. I have assembled you here in order to make you find a remedy for these misfortunes yourselves. But I ask you not to speak of the past, not to discuss who was guilty of the troubles, not to blame each other".

Then he gave the floor to the representatives of both parties. The representatives thanked the viceroy for his efforts and the viceroy left the hall.

The assembly, chaired by General Malama, began a discussion of the issues. The most important and difficult of them was an assurance of security for the Muslims when they moved to the summer pastures and the liquidation of the terrorist and murderous Armenian groups who were the source of all misfortunes.

The Assembly discussed other issues besides the above, but we do not want to take up readers' time and trouble their minds.

Discussion on migration to summer pastures

The fifth session of the Assembly was held on 25 February, and it discussed the migration to summer pastures and the return, as proposed by the Muslims.

Kalantar, editor of the newspaper *Musak* spoke thus: "The problem of moving to the summer pastures and returning is one of the most important issues in the Caucasus, because it concerns not only the nomads, but the whole population. When the move to summer pastures and the return begin, the majority of people come into contact with each other. Even in former days of peace and stability there were small clashes and conflicts when people moved back and forth between the summer and winter pastures.

As we know, hostility has already arisen between the Muslims and Armenians; the origin and occurrence of such clashes are beyond dispute. Bearing this in mind, migration to the summer pastures and back must be banned in order to at least restore peace here, and it is necessary to make it applicable to all migrants, everywhere in our region. The migration of flocks of sheep and cattle to the summer pastures and back is not inherent only in the Caucasus. This problem exists in Europe, too; for example, in Tirol,[29] Switzerland, in the Alps. But we differ greatly from Europe. In Europe people only travel for a few hours, and only the shepherds and animals migrate. But our nomads travel for weeks. For instance, they roam with the sheep and cattle from the district of Javanshir to the districts of Zengezur and Noy Bayazit. This is a distance of over 200 versts. These nomads must inevitably pass Armenian villages. In the past the Muslims and Armenians were friends and lived in peace, but even then there were small offences and disagreements between them over the pastures, theft, fire and other causes. And the government did not do anything serious to remove these discords. It is true that the issue of nomads arose in 1905, the government was against it, and the Governor General of Irevan also protested. But prohibitions did not help and the Governor of Ganja asked for government permission not to allow the nomads to migrate, to make them remain in their winter pastures and camps. In 1861 the viceroy drafted special regulations for the nomads. But this did not meet their needs and did not have any effect.

Several regulations have been introduced recently in the province of Ganja to regulate the migration of nomads to summer and winter pastures. There was also the problem of the veterinarians who controlled the nomads' cattle. They treated the nomads very badly; their aim was to make the nomads abandon migration.

But this has also failed to produce any effect. The nomads are still migrating to and fro. There has been no change because real measures have not been developed yet.

---

[29] Eastern Alpine region in the west of Austria, North of Italy and Switzerland, the Alps.

It is necessary to provide facilities in the nomads' winter camps, to ease their lives there, but the government has not done anything. The Ottomans have done more for their nomads than the Russian government. The Ottomans took a number of measures in 1841 to persuade the nomadic Kurds not to roam to and fro with their sheep and cattle. Nomadic life is very base and undesirable. Only uncivilized tribes are nomads. The whole Caucasus suffers from the nomadic life of the Muslims. Something must be done to persuade them to change from this way of life and economy, to make them live settled lives and to switch to crafts and agriculture. At present, and in some places, the Muslims seem to desire such a life; they cultivate cotton, rice, they are changing gradually to a settled way of life; in many places nomadic life is simply a custom. Nowadays there is no need for migration at all. The government and state should take due measures and help them to begin a settled life. Otherwise, the development of culture in the Caucasus is impossible. For the present, the government should ban migration to the summer pastures. It is necessary to separate these two hostile nations, to put a kind of barrier between them, to restrict contact and make them forget this hostility. Otherwise, there will be clashes again. We say these words not only to benefit the Armenians, but also the Muslims. When people move to the summer pastures in the mountains with small children, they very often suffer from diseases and other maladies and do not know what to do. If there is an accident, or something else, they are unable to do anything, or give help. We, the Armenian representatives, ask you to stop the migration of nomads immediately, for the sake of peace."

> **Author's view**: Mr. Kalantar's speech appears unbiased and logical. But to make the readers aware of this writer's purpose, I would like to add some words. Everybody knows that Mr. Kalantar is for the ending of nomad migration. Because in every province, the Armenians have settled on land close to forests and the summer pastures in the mountains, drinking pure, fresh spring water. But Muslims everywhere have settled on the plains and lowlands. Mr. Kalantar's intention is to

make the Muslims drink water mixed with the urine and waste of their animals in the heat of the summer and perish by and by. Well! This is the helpful advice to us from our Armenian neighbours. Then Mr. Kalantar holds up the Ottomans as an example on the migration of nomads and praises them. Of course, Mr.Editor Kalantar has every right to say this, because the measures taken by the Ottoman in 1844 were also adopted under pressure from the Armenians. Then he recommends the separation of the two nations from each other. Perhaps Mr. Editor shares Mr. Bahadirov's views on this issue.

We said a lot about the separation of the two nations when we described the events in Javanshir and other places.

Ahmed bey Agayev's answer to Mr. Kalantar

"Mr. Kalantar's words contradict the sciences of the humanities, society, progress of nations and the truth which derives from them. All nations have three stages of development:

The first stage is the hunting stage, people live by hunting.

The second is the migration of nomads engaged in cattle-breeding.

The third stage is the cultural stage, when people settle in towns and engage in crafts and the cultivation of agricultural products.

All tribes must experience these three stages.

No decree or action can make people bypass these stages. Progress and the passage of time determine the move from one stage to another. It is a normal and natural process. In other words, the efforts of the government and the state to make the nomads cultural, or civilized, may be likened to changing the north wind into a west wind....

Millions of people live on milk, cheese, meat, wool and other animal products. When Mr. Kalantar says they must give up their nomadic lives, he never considers the problem of what these people will live on. It seems that Mr. Kalantar is ready to victimize so many Muslims for the sake of a handful of Armenians living in those mountainous areas.

It is easy to say stop the migration of nomads, but to show them how and on what to live is difficult. Has Mr. Kalantar ever been among these nomads? Has he ever noticed that at the approach of summer all the animals, people, cows and sheep - all of them - turn their faces towards the mountains and start bleating? Everyone and everything instinctively moves towards the mountains.

It is beyond the power of man to overcome this ignorance. A winter camp becomes a real hell in summer. The pools and rivers dry up, the grass withers, millions of insects rise from the ground and bite every living being like snakes, whenever and wherever they find them. Malaria infects and kills man and animal without distinction. Does Mr.Kalantar want to subject the nomads to these misfortunes? If he means to do just this, then he will be displaying real mercy! This is not true humanitarianism. The government must think first about the winter camps and pastures, supply them with water, plant trees, make other improvements, and then ban the nomads from moving to the mountains in summer and returning in winter. Otherwise, no decree, no order will be of use and the nomads will continue to live in their usual way. Because any order or decree beyond the laws of nature may shorten people's lives, affect their well-being, or cause them great harm. These winter camps and pastures, which become a hell in summer, were prosperous and pleasant provinces in the past, in ancient times.....

They were prosperous and pleasant because of the government's care, because of the measures it implemented. The government constructed underground water reservoirs and improved living conditions, and the people became settled, engaged in commerce and crafts and also in the cultivation of crops. Now the government takes no care of them at all, does nothing to make these lands fit for settled life. Only a nomadic life is possible there. The government has no right or authority to issue a decree and ban people from moving to the summer pastures. Nobody will obey such an unjust decree. We, the innocent and guiltless Muslims, would consider such a decree as a great punishment for us. This could only be done to please the Armenians. And it would by no means help the establishment of peace".

Having spoken these words, he felt dizzy and took to his chair, then he was ushered to another room in the palace and returned to the hall after a while when he had recovered. [30]

When Ahmed bey became dizzy, **Garabey Garabeyov** took up the speech on the same topic: "Mr. Ahmad Agayev said all that was necessary. I can only add that before banning the migration of nomads, the government must improve living conditions in the winter camps so that people may live there in summer. But if migration is banned right now, the Armenian-Muslim conflict may flare up and ignite the whole Caucasus".

Ibrahim Aga Vekilov: "Not only Muslims, but other nationalities are also engaged in cattle-breeding in the Caucasus. But those people, including the Armenians, live a settled life. Therefore, they do not need any help. If the Muslims do not move to the summer pastures, their cattle, as well as themselves, will perish."

Sarkisyan: Heat and thirst are not the reasons. Because other nations do not migrate and they remain in their winter camps; they have arranged their lives well. I believe that the Muslims do not benefit very much from cattle breeding, they would sell their cattle to those who live in the highlands, and they themselves would take up crop cultivation in the lowlands. The elders of the Muslims must promote this among their people".

Muhammad bey Shahmaliyev: "Messrs. Kalantar and Agayev, who spoke before me, gave their views on the migration of nomads. Mr.Kalantar declared the government's opinion on the problem. He wants the migration of nomads to be banned. But he did not cover the whole problem. It is clear from Mr. Agayev's speech that the migration of nomadic Muslims is a historically and theoretically based tradition and custom. This custom will disappear one day, there will be no need for a governmental decree. But I think that such statements deal with only one side of the problem, there is a

---

[30] Ahmed bey Agayev fought assiduously for his nation, and everybody is aware of his patriotism. But I must also say that not everyone appreciates his efforts, although most representatives of our nation have a high and positive opinion about him. He did not get one-hundredth of what he deserved. This means that there are still people of our nationality who are ungrateful by nature (M.S.Ordubadi).

second aspect. It is that not only Muslims are engaged in cattle breeding here, the people of Dagestan, Zagatala, Samur, Teyvant and other places are also cattle-breeders, and they benefit very much from their sheep and cattle. Not only the population of these lands, but also those of the afore-mentioned places benefit: from their neighbours' woven carpets, kilims and other articles of that kind. If they give up cattle-breeding, they will lose their source of income, their current occupation provides a living, and they live by their cattle-breeding. My request to the assembly is not to speak about banning migration, but about how to ease the process of migration for nomads. It is clearly possible that there will be conflicts between these two nations when the nomads move to the summer pastures and return to their winter pastures and camps. Therefore, the government and we must try to fulfil the task set before us and discuss how to carry it out"

Hajiyev: "We have not assembled here to demonstrate our skills in oratory, to discuss the principles of administration in Switzerland, or in Europe. Of course, it is good to be like Europe. But we must take decisions here on this problem. The migration will start in a month's time. We must try to solve the problem, to take decisions."

General Malama, chairman of the assembly: "Gentlemen! I see that if we continue like this, we shall hear many opinions, but nothing concrete. I ask you to speak concretely, about what decisions to take".

Peterson (secretary in the viceroy's office): "Mr. Viceroy is giving special attention to this problem. But the views expounded here are of a theoretical nature, there is nothing constructive about them".

General Malama's final words on the migration issue: "It is impossible to ban migration. If a nation has become accustomed to something, we cannot ban it immediately; it is only possible to persuade the nation to relinquish this custom gradually, by and by".

The floor was then taken by Ziyadkhanov, followed by Topchubashov. When the Armenians saw that their attempt to adopt a decision on the banning of migration had failed, their representatives Khatisov and Avetisov spoke in chorus. Finally, General Malama read out the decision of the assembly and concluded its work:

"First of all, let no one obstruct the migration of nomads this year. Secondly, it is necessary to call two assemblies, let the first one discuss the issue of this year's migration, the next one - the future of this issue, in this way enabling the nomads to change to a settled mode of life".

Thus, the assembly finished its work and a decision to ban migration by Muslim nomads was not adopted.

The sixth session of peace negotiations between the Armenians and Muslims in the Viceroy's Palace on 28 February

The assembly began its work with General Malama in the chair. First there was much discussion about the migration of nomads, then about Article 7 of the programme submitted by the Muslims. The Article read: "It is necessary to create the conditions for government officials to perform their responsibilities in peace and without fear".

General Malama: "Who wants to speak about this?"

Ahmed bey Agayev, who had been sitting silently in the hall for several minutes, rose to his feet and said:

"For several years, we, the population of the Caucasus, have been experiencing a strange life, living in strange conditions. One group of people keeps everybody in fear. Nobody is allowed, nobody is given a chance to disclose his thoughts, develop his work or explain his opinion. Those in charge of the people's affairs and government officials live in constant fear. If a man dares to disclose his views openly, or if an official fulfils his duty honestly, he receives death threats. It is impossible to live like this! It is necessary to put an end to it. Some officials and men of high position have become very base and mean because of the letters they receive threatening them with death; they have lost their compassion and sense of responsibility for their work. Through fear they incline towards those who send these threatening letters, they commit injustices and are merciless towards the other party. If things continue like this, it will be impossible to live at all. They call such things terror and justify themselves. But one can only tolerate terror up to a certain point. If it is forbidden to speak or to write one's views openly in the country, then it is admissible to commit violence against the oppressor and the ruthless in order to liberate people from oppression and violence, in order to serve humanity. When terror reaches such a level, it is impossible to display patience and tolerate it.

If terror compels a government official not to serve the nation honestly, according to his own conscience and fairly, then there will be no freedom, justice or equality in our province. At present most government officials, perhaps all of them, bow to the terrorist detachments and seek to please the terrorists, in this way they commit violence, oppression, injustice and other iniquities upon the other party.

We, the Muslims, will not tolerate this state of affairs any longer. And we declare here openly that if the situation remains like this, if the terrorist groups and detachments continue to rampage in the Caucasus, peace and stability will not be ensured. We do not preach against anyone. But for the sake of peace we want to focus the attention of the assembly on this problem and say that the majority of government officials and judges in the Caucasus are afraid of Armenian terror and do not work fairly or with compassion. From fear, these officials do nothing to restore peace and stability; they practise oppression, impatience and injustice on one party, remaining blind to the misdeeds and injustice of the other. And so there will never be peace and order here."

Peterson: "This is not the time or place for such words. This issue must not be discussed here at all". (The Armenians cheer loudly).

Ahmed bey Agayev: "May Mr. Peterson excuse me. The Assembly is just the place for such words.

We were invited here to discuss our problems and considerations openly, perhaps some people do not like it, but that is not our concern. And our goal in discussing the problem is to reveal to the whole of Russia the names of those officials who have forgotten their honour and conscience, bravery and courage, who have become obedient through fear of death threats; our goal is to tell of their misdeeds, injustice and vile actions. Perhaps then these officials will regain their conscience and display some valour".

Karbalayi Israfil Hajiyev: "I do not know why so many exceptions are made for the Armenians. We know that they are Christians, rich and cultured, and share the same religion as the Russians. As if all this is not enough, they must also have their terror groups!! We could also commit outrages. We could also have Mauser rifles and bombs, and use them. We could also murder high officials and governors better than the Armenians. But we do not do any of this. Because it is base and mean, it does not suit our nation.

Our aim in the discussion of this issue is to make the government do its work, perform its duties, execute justice properly and without fear. If the government does not do this, then we shall also be compelled to resort to terrorism."

These speeches by Ahmed bey Agayev and Karbalayi Israfil Hajiyev impressed the hall very much. They spoke of cases of government officials and men in high positions receiving death threats by mail. The Armenian representatives began noisily expressing their dissatisfaction.

Ispandaryan, editor of the newspaper *Nurdar*: "We will leave the hall. We cannot stay to hear your denunciations...!"

Karbalayi Haji Israfil: "If you wish, you may go! Nobody is going to beg you to stay".

Tagiyanosov: "No, no, I do not agree with my comrade Ispandaryan. We must stay and hear the words of our Muslim comrades. We also do not want terrorism in our province, and we also do not want people in office to commit injustices through fear of terror, we do not want them to punish and oppress people arbitrarily. But I ask you to explain everything so that we can understand what you mean".

Shahmaliyev: "You, the Armenians, know that we have not gathered here to praise and eulogize the government. We have come here to speak openly, to say that because of the fear of terror, government officials support the Armenians. Such a situation can not be tolerated and can not continue henceforward.

Besides, such things also influence the Muslims. Our people also think of terrorizing government officials, of threatening them in order to make them work honestly, fairly. It is our duty to tell you that there will be no peace while there is terror".

Arutyunov: "We have assembled here to achieve peace. We can not, and it will not, help achieve peace if the Muslims raise this problem. Where and when have government officials oppressed the Muslims through fear of terror? For my own part, I can say that I have not witnessed such a thing. We must not engage here in denunciation. We are not gendarmes. There are gendarmes in other places and so we must not speak about this here at all".

Alimardan bey Topchubashov: "We cannot close our eyes and remain blind. Our situation makes us raise this question. The situation in our country is that government officials and civil servants are unable to work fairly and honestly. Of course they do not pay much attention to threatening letters and fear in high government offices. But low level officials in the provinces fear such letters and are not able to perform their duties honestly. How are they guilty?

When you ask them: "Why do you do such things?" They answer:

"We are frightened, we also have our families!"

We say that there must be a situation, an atmosphere in which officials are not frightened, do not commit injustices and work honestly".

Kalantar: "We, the Armenians, do not understand the Muslims' words at all. They complain either about the army, or the newspapers, or the government, or about dismissing Armenian soldiers. They also demand the closure of some parties, or talk about fear of terror and parties. We could also say a lot, but we do not do so, because good people must not speak of some things at all. Such things have nothing to do with the problem we are discussing now. Let us move on to the main subject".

General Malama: "Let us, let us move on!"

Adil Khan Ziyadkhanov: "No, we must not. We must first solve the problem. We have assembled here for peace. It is impossible to achieve peace by making official speeches. Everybody must say what is in in his heart. The Armenian representatives speak of sneaking and denunciation. We are not afraid of such slanders. We want to achieve peace whole-heartedly and devotedly, it is our duty to disclose everything that obstructs the achievement of peace. One of them is terror. The Armenians tell us to indicate the remedies to root out terrorism. We can not identify the remedies. They must look themselves. If the government does not find a remedy, hence our Muslims will at least be innocent before their own consciences".

An Armenian representative from Irevan: "The Muslims also have their own parties and detachments. Doesn't the Deli Ali* detachment frighten and horrify the government? The Muslims must also liquidate this detachment".

Ahmed bey Agayev: "When we raised the issue of terrorism, we did it only for the sake of peace and order. We did it because the Muslims of the Caucasus think that there will be no peace or order while there is terrorism. We are obliged to express our nation's view here openly. But they, the Armenians here, call us denouncers and spies, let them say so. The whole world knows who the denouncers and spies are. Besides, I am very often asked how long it will be possible to tolerate terror and exercise patience towards it.

In my previous speech I gave a clear answer, and declared that if the free expression of thought is not allowed in the country, then it is possible to countenance terror. If such terror serves the whole population and mankind; for instance, when terror saved the people and the province from a ruthless and brutal ruler in the Caucasus, when it helped to restore people's trampled rights and authorities, we all called upon such terror to help. But after some time the terror overstepped its limits, changed its goals and began to defend the interests of only one side, one party. It forced the officials, civil servants and men with credit and authority among the population to ignore justice, compassion and to satisfy the interests of only one

---

*This does not match the reality. Facts prove that Deli Ali's actions were stabilizing factors during the "Armenian-Muslim Clashes". See Tiflis leaflet, from 25 August 1905.

party, one side. It is impossible to tolerate such a state, to exercise patience towards terror. For example, we have assembled here to discuss how to achieve peace, to find ways and concrete means. But to put them into practice, to realise them, is the duty of the province's rulers. If these rulers, that is, those upon whom the government has laid the responsibility of administrating the province, are in fear of terror, will they lead a fight against it? If they even begin to do so, they will always incline towards the terroriser, support it and oppress and threaten the other party.

And it is obvious that the oppressed party will always be discontented and will remain hostile and irreconcilable. And there will be no peace. This is why we raise the issue of terror. We say: if you really want peace, you must also try to put an end to terror, together with other evil actions. In response we are told that we are speaking of the Dashnaksutyun Party. We were not thinking of that at all. We demand an end to terror. And the Armenians immediately think of Dashnaksutyun. It seems that Dashnaksutyun is connected with terror. But I repeat again that we are not concerned with Dashnaksutyun. We do not mean Dashnaksutyun! But yesterday Mr. Khatisov, in his eloquent, but also provocative, speech said that Dashnaksutyun serves the ideas and goals of the great men of Russia, its generals, even those of the Viceroy of the Caucasus. It was founded 15 years ago, it has its own troops, treasury and soldiers. We, the representatives of Muslims, were very much surprised to hear this and began to think to ourselves: if this is true, if there is an armed party which has been functioning for 15 years, the government is aware of it and does nothing about it, then that means that the government shares that party's values, is in accord with it. It is useless on our part to demand that the government and the Armenians close, or liquidate, such a party. Then we must take care of ourselves and look for remedies for our problems. Then we must also organize armed groups. We must also have our own parties, similar to Dashnaksutyun. If the government tolerates the misdeeds of one side, it must tolerate those of the other side, too, otherwise there will be chaos and anarchy in the country".

General Malama: "No! No! The government is determined to take serious measures to liquidate such parties, be it Dashnaksutyun or other parties; all such parties have no future, they will be closed".

Muslim representatives: "Bravo! Bravo!"

Karbalayi Israfil Hajiyev: "We want the government to tell us openly whether it is possible to have a state within a state. Is it possible to allow a tribe, or people, which is the subject of the state, to establish parties and create its own troops?! They say that such detachments exist in France and in England. If it is possible for a people to have its own troops, then let us know about it, too. Then we shall think about where to go, because we are civilians and are not able to fight against armed troops. If you want us to obey the decrees of another government, let us know, and we will look for a remedy".

Arutyunov: "When I see the behaviour of the Muslim representatives, I see that they want to attack us, they accuse us. We are on the defensive".

Adil Khan Ziyadkhanov: "We do not attack anybody. We speak openly and truly only because of peace, for the sake of peace".

General Malama: "That is enough discussion. As regards terrorism, we must adopt decisions and oblige the government to take serious measures to liquidate terrorism and armed parties".

The assembly adopted this decision by a majority of votes.

> **Addition**: The Armenians' participation in the assembly was not dictated by a desire to achieve peace, but to defeat the Muslims in a battle of words in the presence of government officials and, later, to ask for more benefits and compensation for damage. Therefore, they made much ado in the presence of General Malama. The Armenian representatives Khatisov, Arutyunov and Arakelyan made long speeches about damages at the eighth session of the assembly. The government was aware of the Armenians' desire, which was impossible to fulfil, therefore, it responded many times: "We do not want to poke into the past".

Armenian Ambitions in the Peace Assembly and Newspaper Attacks on Muslims

Here is an article published on 12 February 1906, in Tiflis, in the Armenian newspaper *Araj*, as proof that the above-named Armenian representatives took part in the peace assembly with quite different motives:

"Peace and the Sunni Muslims"

The Armenian-Muslim conflicts have been going on for perhaps a year now; villages and towns are being burnt and destroyed. Men, women and children are suffering and dying of hunger. Several districts across the whole province are being burnt and resemble hell.

Bloody storms strengthen and then subside, small destructive currents rage. And so far nobody knows when these events will end. When will these clashes and conflicts, which have turned our dear land into a hell, stop and be silenced? We hear very often about the bloody truth and the moans and cries: "Armistice! Armistice!" Both enemies call upon their leaders, the clerics, to try to achieve this armistice, to hold assemblies, to set up peace commissions. They make speeches, call for peace and kiss each other. But the kiss of armistice turns into the kiss of riot. The storm rages again. Armaments again begin to echo. The groans and shrieks of the innocent victims are heard. The bloody events spread to new areas, moving from village to village, from town to town.

Now, after all this, the Viceroy of the Caucasus has issued a decree on the forming of a commission. This commission will be large in number and will cover the whole Caucasus. Of course, it is clear that nobody can say anything against the decisions of this commission. But when the goals of the commission change and are substituted by something different, it is like a building that loses its original architecture and ornamentation. The changes, and conditions in the commission, give one reason to believe that it will be no different from its predecessors.

It should be mentioned in particular that this commission will consist not only of persons elected by the common people, but also of well-known national leaders, beys, khans, landlords and pan-Islamist ideologists. These very men have been the initiators of the Muslim attacks. In addition there is another reason, the reverse side of the problem. If we penetrate to its depths, we shall see that it is more dangerous and harmful. Besides the representatives of the Armenians and Shiite Muslims, the representatives of the Sunni Muslims will also take part in the commission. We are against the organization of the commission in this form, because the issue is being presented as if the Armenian-Muslim riots have emerged due to national and religious hostility and not as part of events current across the whole of Russia; the consequences of the conflict affect not only the Armenians and Muslims, but the whole Caucasus. The lands where the Armenian-Muslim riots take place remind us of the Vendean[31] events in France. To quell the peasant insurrections (1793-1796) against the French Revolutionary government, an assembly was held in which representatives of all tribes participated. But here in the peace assembly, everybody has not been represented: not all the hostile parties, or the Russians and Georgians, who live here in great number, have been represented. Then another question arises: why are the Sunni Muslims offended? Why are they represented in the Assembly? The Muslim representatives think that the Sunnis are also Muslims, like the Shiites, therefore, they will also be hostile to the Armenians. This idea is wrong from the outset, because the Sunnis have always been neutral and have not taken part in the Shiites' looting raids.

Even if they have sometimes taken part in them, they have done so out of humanitarianism and under the influence of feuds. If one believes that the Armenians are fighting against all the Muslims of the Caucasus, this is wrong and far from the truth. The Armenians do not conceal feelings of hostility in their hearts and have lived side by side with the Muslims for many years. And even now when

---

[31] Vendean- perhaps Vendee is meant. This is a department of France on the shore of the Atlantic Ocean. At the end of the 18th and the beginning of the 19th century Vendee was the centre of counter-revolutionary rioting, known in history as the Vendean Wars.

the Armenians take to arms against their neighbours, they do it with pain in their hearts. They do it only to defend themselves. The Armenians do not want to fight with the Sunnis, nor with peaceful Shiites. Dashnaksutyun is a revolutionary party which unites Armenian fighters; under the party banner its members try to achieve an armistice. By word and deed they propagate friendship between the conflicting tribes. In this light, it is an injustice to make the Sunni representatives sit together with the Shiites and oppose them to the Armenian representatives.

If the Sunnis take part in the commission, then our other neighbours - the Russians and Georgians - must also be represented there. But if you believe that they are also hostile to the Armenians, like the Muslims, this is wrong and groundless. If the Muslim representatives do not as, usual, obstruct the work of the commission with their intrigues, then the Armenian representatives must draw attention to this misunderstanding and illuminate it"

Signature: Y.T

Painful Events in Gatar

This chapter is about the tragic events which took place on 29 July 1906, in the village of Gatar in the province of Zengezur, in administration area 5 (based on letters from reporters).

Renaissance or primordialism

We gave detailed information when we wrote about the events in Okhchu-Sabadak, nevertheless, I think it necessary to say something further. I do this because I want readers to know that Armenian intelligence did its utmost to possess the said administration area five. They wanted to destroy the Muslim villages located along the road which led from Irevan to Nakhchivan, combine the Armenians of Irevan with their armed forces in Nakhchivan, destroy the Muslim villages located along the road from Nakhchivan to Zengezur and combine the Armenian volunteers of Zengezur with their armed forces in Nakhchivan.

To do this it was necessary to destroy the villages of Okhchu and Shabadak, which were key to administration area five. Thus they began to assemble in the Armenian villages of Barabatum and Chekedek after their defeat in Shusha, in order to regroup their armed forces scattered at Javanshir and Jabrail. The real goal in mobilizing their soldiers and regrouping the army was to discourage the Muslims living in the village of Gatar and to prevent them from assisting Muslims affected by the tragic events took place in Okhchu and Shabadak. To realise their dreams, they appointed an Armenian by the name of Mirza Aram as commander of the armed forces assembled there and ordered him to start the offensive.

Aram's initiative

On 29 July 1906, with the consent of Mirza Aram, Safiyar bey, the servant of Jamal bey, a nobleman and hereditary bey from the dynasty of Ulkhu, resident in the village of Garachemen, was invited to the Madan Bazaar on the pretext of shopping. This poor Safiyar bey, unaware of the Armenians' plan and unarmed, mounted his horse and set out for the bazaar. Dashnaksutyun murderers ambushed him in the gardens and killed him cruelly. When news of his murder reached the Muslims of the nearby villages, they attacked the bazaar, killed an Armenian and set an abandoned copper mine on fire.

The uproar from the incident shook the villages in the Gapan Gorge. Armenian volunteers and armed detachments attacked the bazaar, set the Muslim shops on fire and inflicted damage worth half a million manats. The merchants of Ordubad, whose goods had been looted, found shelter in the village of Gatar. When the tragedy took place in Gatar, six Muslims escaped and reached the slopes of Okhchu and Shabadak, where they were murdered by the Armenians. On 29 July, after the destruction of the bazaar in Madan, the Armenians attacked the village of Karkhana and began shooting at it.

News of Karkhana

Following the destruction and looting of the bazaar in Madan, at about 12 o'clock on 29 July 1906, the Armenians attacked the village of Karkhana. They fired at the village from all sides. The inhabitants of this village were poor and humble and, therefore, did not have modern rifles. They defended the village for several minutes, but could not resist the Armenians, who fired from 1500 rifles simultaneously. They retreated and scattered into the bushes. The Armenians found them one by one and murdered them or took them captive. Once they found about 30 women and children, and also unarmed men, hiding behind a rock. Among them was a young woman by the name of Pakiza, who had a suckling baby girl, Firuza, in her arms (her husband Tahir from Ordubad had been killed in the clashes). Frightened by the sound of shooting, the poor baby was crying bitterly. Afraid that the Armenians would hear the baby's cries, the men took the baby from her mother by force and closed its mouth so that the Armenians would not hear it. As a result the poor child died. Very few of the residents of Karkhana remained alive.

Five villages destroyed

After slaughtering the residents of Karkhana, on the same day, in the afternoon, the Armenians also destroyed the villages listed below. These villages had not prepared defences, therefore the residents left them without a fight.

The villages destroyed were: Lov, Khalaj, Injevar and Dashnov. The surviving inhabitants of these villages found shelter in the village of Gatar. The people of this village were good fighters. They did not give the Armenians a chance to lift their heads from their shelters.

The battle of Gatar

At about 12 o'clock on 1 August, the Armenians surrounded Gatar on all sides and began shooting at it. At this very moment police chief Sakharov and several policemen were in the village. The skirmish escalated with each passing hour. A policeman by the name of Jalil, Lezghin by nationality, who was there at the time, turned to Sakharov and said: "Mr. Chief of Police, don't you have any compassion? Don't you see how they are pouring fire onto the Muslims?" "I cannot defend the Muslims, don't you see how well the Armenians are shooting?[32]

---

[32] When you look through the pages of the newspapers from 1904, you see how the Muslim peasants suffer everywhere from the police chiefs and other high officials of the provinces. And the Muslims' defeat in the village of Gatar is connected with the name of Sakharov, the police chief. I hope that the Muslims remember till the Day of Judgement the words uttered by Sakharov: "I cannot defend the Muslims, don't you see how well the Armenians are shooting?"

The Armenians tried hard to destroy the village by breaking into it, but being unaware of the Muslim forces there, they did not dare do so. They consulted Sakharov and, with his consent, they sent 50 Cossacks and one sergeant to ascertain the strength of the Muslim forces.[33]

The Cossacks saw that everybody in the village was armed. "Do not worry and do not respond to Armenian fire. The government itself will punish them". In this way they deceived the Muslims. The Cossacks spread through the village, learned all about the Muslim forces and returned to Sakharov. When he was leaving, the chief of a nomad tribe, whose tribe had come to Gatar out of fear, sent a message to Sakharov asking him to ensure the security of his tribe and to let them leave the village under the protection of the Cossacks, Sakharov refused to help him. According to him, it was better for them to stay in the village and be murdered. After the Cossacks had informed the Armenians about the Muslims' war preparations in the village and left, the Armenians attacked the village from all four sides. Police chief Sakharov, the peace mediator, retreated to the Armenian village of Barabatum with the Cossacks. He climbed to a hilltop and watched the battle through binoculars.

"Bravo, bravo, how well the Armenians attack the village!" His words were heard by a private. The Muslims had not seen such terrible battles before; thus they had never given priority to defence. Not only did the Armenians outnumber the Muslims, which frightened and horrified them, but Gatar was also surrounded by Armenian villages on all four sides, thus every Armenian volunteer could take his rifle and reach the battlefield within ten minutes. If one really looks at the geographical location of Gatar, then he will

---

[33] It is a principle of warfare that the attacking party first tries to learn about the forces and preparations of the enemy, even if it is superior in strength, therefore, it begins a battle with a reconnaissance force, that is, not with intensive fire. The enemy fights like this until the evening, but at night sends reconnaissance detachments to get intelligence. Depending on the size of the enemy about 50 mounted men are sent for this purpose. In this way they get the necessary information about the enemy force. Spies in disguise, or information from captured soldiers, are also used, then they inform the commander by telegram or letter. Then the commander sends sufficient forces to defeat the enemy. Lower level officers do the same. This was the Armenians' intention in Gatar.

admire the valour and courage of the Muslims. As we have already mentioned, Gatar is surrounded by Armenian villages on all sides, it was impossible for its inhabitants to leave the village or get support from other Muslim villages. They could only contact the outside world through the post office located in the Madan bazaar and, unfortunately, police chief Sakharov had had the post office closed and moved to the Armenian village of Barabatum. It became clear that the Muslims of Gatar were besieged by the enemy and they lost hope of getting any support. There was fierce skirmishing in Gatar for nine days but, owing to the bravery and valour of the Muslims, the enemy could not occupy the village. By the end of the battle the Muslims learned that the number of Armenians attacking them was about 8,000. They lost all hope of survival and were heart-broken. Seeking rescue and help they wrote a letter and gave 25 roubles to a messenger to take it to the beys and nobility of Zangilan,[34] asking them for assistance.

"We can not render any assistance to you, seek the remedy yourself," was the reply sent to Gatar. This disheartened the Muslims even more. We must also say that the people of Gatar and the village itself suffered greatly at the hands of the Iranian Muslims who worked in Melik Azaryans' copper mine. These merciless Iranian workers rushed into the village with oil barrels and explosives on their backs, crying loudly the name of Ali, the holy Imam of the Muslims. The residents of the village thought that they were bringing ammunition for their Muslim brothers and let them into the village. These ruthless Iranians sprayed the houses with oil, set them on fire and blew up stone buildings with the dynamite.

On the ninth day of the battle, at about 12 o'clock, the Armenians approached the village from all sides, with the intention of occupying it. The Muslim volunteers left the shelters and attacked the enemy. They were sure that the Armenians wanted to

---

[34] As the esteemed reporter says, if only 20 mounted Muslims had fired at the Armenian village of Barabatum from the height behind it, then the Armenians might have turned to that direction and the Muslims would have had a chance to break the siege, repulse the attack and end their misfortune. Alas, the beys and nobility of Zangilan displayed no honesty or love for their nation

occupy the village and slaughter all its inhabitants. The Muslim youth there were already certain of death. Therefore, saying "Better to die on the attack than in a shelter", they fought violently, frequently leaving the shelters to attack the enemy. In this way the battle continued until evening. Then fate began to betray the Muslims by and by, a depression came over them, they felt isolated and disoriented. At night they left the shelters and trenches, went home and fell into the sleep of oblivion. They did not even leave guards around the village that night. The Armenians then occupied the most significant positions around the village. Thus was determined the fate of the village of Gatar.

The Armenians surrounded the village so closely and tightly that there remained no space for even a bird to fly from the siege.[35]

An hour before dawn the Armenians began to fire fiercely at the village. They were also assisted by the Cossacks in the Armenian village of Barabatum. They divided their forces info four and marched on the village. The Iranian workers of Madan, with oil barrels on their backs and dynamite in their hands, walked in front of each of these detachments.[36]

---

[35] The thoughts of a poor Muslim who had found shelter in the village of Khalaj. He wanted to enter the village of Gatar on the night of 9 August: "When I passed the Madan bazaar and reached the village of Gatar I saw a strange scene. Clouds of smoke had covered the village. No light from a lantern, fire or match was seen. No sound from animals, insects or men was heard, the village was lost in darkness, there was a deep and terrible silence in that horrible night. From time to time there came a sound which resembled the cry of a suckling baby; it meant that the residents were not asleep. And sometimes I heard heart-rending cries, as if people were bidding farewell to their native land. I had quite forgotten myself. Tragic cries, mixed with the natural silence of the night, and hate echoed in the mountains. The mountain ranges around sat embracing their knees like mothers weeping for their dead sons. I listened very hard, the low cries of mothers at dawn confused me. I walked in fear and horror not thinking of myself. Where? I did not know! I came to abandoned Muslim shelters and trenches. They were full of empty water jugs and cartridges piled in heaps. The smell of powder which rose from the rock and stones stung my nostrils. When I saw the Armenians from afar standing ready for the occupation of the village, I began to run towards the village of Kelledag."

[36] What is strange is the behaviour of the Iranian workers who have always been tortured and murdered by the Armenians, nevertheless, they helped the Armenians everywhere. There is a proverb which goes like this: "A clever enemy is better than a foolish friend".

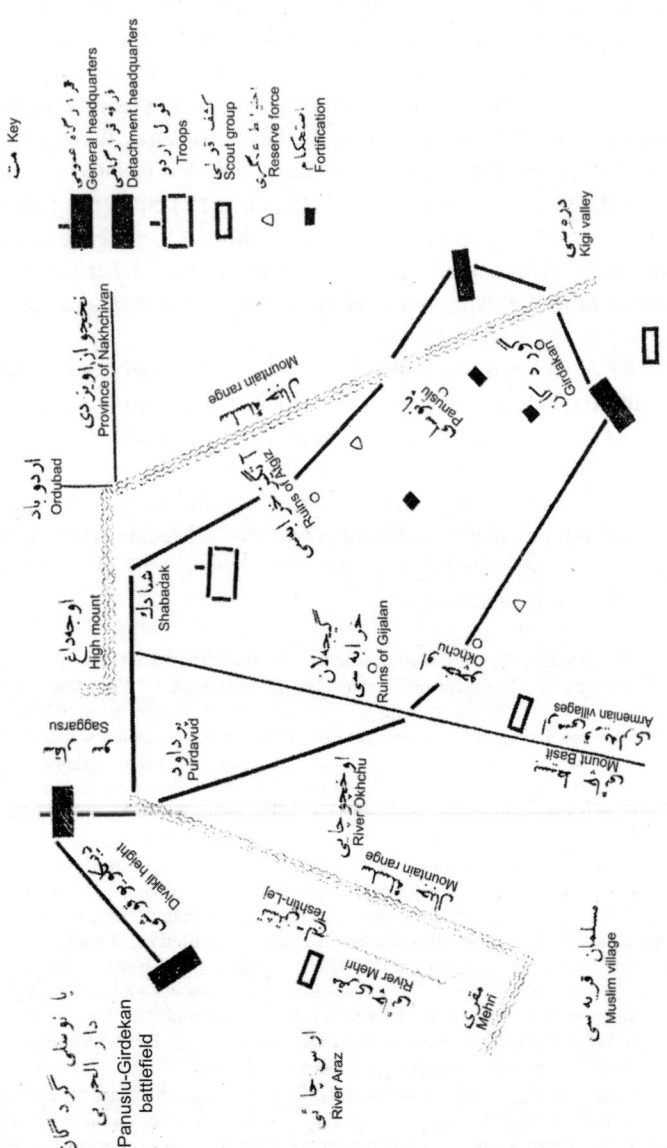

They were to set the houses on fire and blow them up. The Muslims of the village were certain of defeat, but emerged from the battle victorious. Although the Armenians attacked several times, each time they suffered great losses and were obliged to retreat, then they reinforced their ranks from the reserve in the rear. Despite their great losses, they rose to their feet and rushed into the village. The battle raged fiercely, the enemies shed each other's blood with guns and daggers. The horrifying shrieks of the Armenians, the tumult of guns and other arms, the loud cries of the Muslim volunteers calling on God for help and the wailing of mothers on the rooftops mingled, making it seem like Doomsday. The smoke from the rifles and guns rising to the sky and the dust mixed with blood thrown up by the horses' hooves hovered like clouds of misfortune over the village. Under these clouds the representatives of the two nations were waging a life or death struggle: one of them maddened by the lust of national ambition, the other not thinking of life any more. The battle was like a spring torrent in which the currents thrash and tangle with each other. This bloody fight, which had broken out at dawn, continued until evening. The Armenians and the Muslims fought in confusion. Although the village was completely burnt out, the Muslims were not eager to leave: "Better to perish and remain in the fatherland, than to roam the deserts in thirst and hunger". By the evening the Armenians were exploding bombs to frighten the Muslims. They damaged the houses, but could not make the residents leave the village. In the evening, after the Armenians had retreated, the Muslims understood that it was impossible to stay in the village any longer. At night they left the village and walked towards the village of Kelledag.

Summary of events

The organizer of the battle in the village of Gatar was the Armenian leader Aram, who had inflicted great harm on the Muslims. The siege began on 29 July 1906 and continued until 9 August. Iranian workers openly helped the Armenians. The leader of the Iranian workers was a man by the name of Suleyman, from the village of Astamal in the province of Garadagh; he helped the Armenians very much. The village of Gatar was completely burnt out in the battle, but the residents did not leave. When the Muslims finally did abandon it and it was destroyed, the Armenians launched the battle of Okchu-Shabadak.

Events in Okhchu-Shabadak and Gapan Gorge

Only in Shusha could the politics of the Armenian intelligence associations flourish in the province of Ganja. These associations carried out various oppressions and brutalities against the Muslims in Shusha, torturing the residents of the Muslim villages and humiliating them in ways incompatible with principles of humanity. There were countless such acts of violence and humiliation. The Muslims believed that the first virtue of humanity was patience and so they did not respond to these actions at once, in order not to spoil good neighbourly relations. But the Armenians claimed that because of the failure of the Great Russian Revolution they had not been able to accomplish their cause, and so they challenged the Muslims to battle. When the Muslims became aware of the Armenians' insidious intentions and that they were going to organize troubles and disorder in various quarters of the town, they began to act. Being brave and fearless from birth, the residents of Shusha took preventive measures and acted first, and did not refrain from punishing the Armenians.

The Armenians were completely defeated. They sent telegrams to all corners of the country about their defeat. This caused great disappointment among the Armenian intelligence associations and politicians. They then turned their faces towards Zengezur and sent their envoys to mobilize soldiers in Irevan, Abaran and Alexandropol for the fight for Hayastan (Armenia). They prepared for battle, drew up plans and mobilized soldiers to wage war in Zengezur. Shusha was not the right place to make preparations for fighting in Zengezur; it was not easy to send fire-arms there after the Armenian defeat.

Thus the Armenians were doing their best to send arms, ammunition and soldiers from Irevan to other places for future battles.

In those days the Armenians were a little stronger along the road from Irevan to Zengezur. Taking advantage, their leaders issued orders to their army commanders to exert pressure on the Muslim villages located along the road. They were trying to create a road to victory from Irevan to Zengezur, oppressing the villages along the road and in the mountain passes. Many villages were destroyed, many houses fell.

The villages of Khanlilar and Itgiranlar were destroyed; the tragedies in the province of Nakhchivan and the settlement of Jahri occurred swiftly. And it became clear that government troops were acting jointly with the Armenians against the Muslims. On the other hand, they were not able to physically destroy the Muslim villages of Dirnis, Unus and Pezmeri in order to get to Zengezur through the mountains, and so they subjected them to psychological pressure.

After the terror enacted against the above-mentioned villages, the goal was to capture Zengezur. But the villages of Okhchu-Shabadak, Purdavud and Aguz blocked Armenian progress, because the residents of those Muslim villages were very brave and good fighters. They had good relations with each other and lived in the harmony which is sacred for every Muslim.

All these villages were key to the province of Zengezur. The Armenians had studied the Muslim villages, with the help of their spies and engineers, and made military preparations for their complete destruction. The Armenian military forces gathered in Gapan Gorge, began the fighting and reported regularly on developments to the leaders who ruled them. Besides the volunteers from Irevan, regular troops also came from Alexandropol, Abaran and Shuragel, and began to manoeuvre in the Armenian villages of Agulis, Kelagi and Demgurt, waiting for the battle to start. In addition, the regular Armenian troops, defeated and discouraged in Shusha, were revived and supplied with arms and ammunition around Agdam, they were reinforced and sent towards Gatar, where the copper mines were situated. This was done with the intention of diverting the attention of the brave residents of Gatar, who were ready to sacrifice their lives, and not to allow them to help Okhchu. The Armenian forces which had been defeated in Shusha assembled near the copper mine on 20 June and were placed under the command of an Armenian by the name of Aram Nehramov. The Armenian military forces were located in two important spots: around the copper mine and in the Armenian village of Agulis; and also in nearby Armenian villages at distances of four or five versts from Ordubad. On 4 August 1906, the commander of the Armenian troops in Agulis, Ashot by name, received a written order from Irevan to assemble his forces in the villages of Panuslu and Girdekan in the neighbourhood of Okhchu-Shabadak. On 7 August the Agulis troops assembled in Panuslu. The troops at the copper mine near Gatar also received an order from their central headquarters in Shusha to assemble in Panuslu, but as the battle in Gatar had reached a critical stage, they only arrived at the village of Panuslu on 8 August. When the two armies combined in Panuslu, the military preparations and supplies were complete. On 9 August, the Armenians began to build fortifications on hilltops around the four Muslim villages, whose residents were completely unaware of what was happening.

The battle of Okhchu-Shabadak, or the battlefield

On 9 August 1906, when the residents of the four previously mentioned Muslim villages were working in their fields, they saw soldiers building fortifications on the hilltops around the villages, they did not guess that they were Armenians. Various rumours began to spread among the people. They sent several men there to learn what was going on. They saw that military flags were hoisted on the summits of the hills. "They are government flags", they thought and blithely continued to walk in that direction. When they got within range of the fortifications, the Armenians fired at them. They understood that the men firing at them were Armenians, they returned home, repaired and prepared their old rifles and stood ready to meet the enemy.

The Armenians had the most update rifles and other armaments. Besides, the Muslims were farmers mainly engaged in the cultivation of crops, thus they were unable to defend the village properly and the most significant positions were occupied by the Armenians. The men in the village were confused by the wailing and moaning of the women because of the approaching crisis. The small children in the village, used to hearing only the roaring and bleating of animals, were shrieking in their cradles and pulling at their mothers' collars; when the trumpets sounded and the enemy firing began, it was as if the Day of Judgement was approaching. The cries of the children and the bleating of the animals mixed and mingled with the sound of shooting which rained down on the Muslims. There was such confusion; as if the horn of Israfil was sounding the warning of doomsday.[37]

The crash of the Armenians' Mauser rifles and the shrieks of the Muslim volunteers attacking the enemy trenches echoed through the Okhchu-Shabadak mountain range, the echoes re-echoing from the peak of the Rocky Mountains and thundering so loudly that nothing else could be heard. The Armenians fired continuously from their trenches. As the Muslims' shots did not always hit the enemy, the Armenians rose from the trenches from time to time to attack. The Muslims ignored the intensive fire from the Armenians and attacked them fearlessly.

When the Armenians saw the bravery and courage of their enemy, they threw explosives from the trenches and shook the Muslims greatly, but their commanders were not perturbed, they encouraged the youth with stirring words and their own example, and in this way restored wavering spirits; they again rushed into attack against the enemy. When the situation was quite critical, the Muslims appealed for help to neighbouring villages, but all roads out of the siege were closed, therefore the Muslims of the village of Okhchu fought and resisted alone for four days. The Armenians were repulsed and they retreated to the Armenian village of Hijalan,

---

[37] According to religious stories, Israfil is one of the angels who will sound his horn to warn everybody of the approach of Doomsday.

where they began to build fortifications and prepare for a new attack. The Muslims pursued the Armenians and a bloody fight ensued. It continued until nightfall, the Armenians were defeated and the village of Hijalan - a new battleground for the Armenians - was completely destroyed.

The fate of Okhchu, or the defeat of the Muslims. 14 August 1906

The Hijalan battle ended with the crushing of the Armenians on 13 August 1906. On 11 August, two days before the end, their commanders had felt in danger of defeat and had called up the reserves remaining from the battle in Gatar and sent messengers to nearby Armenian villages to mobilise more volunteers. Volunteers arrived to help the Armenians from the villages of Layj, Tashtin, Veng, Karlur, Gurasan, Mehri, Asadazur, Girchivan, Agarak, Bahrvar, Ujanabus, (from administration area five), from Karavat, Barabatum, Chekedek, Kudkum, Bagaburj, Chemen, Bukh (from administration area four), Okhaduz, Rakhdakhana, Norashen, Khotanan, Usereng, Sahadur, Chin, Melek, Chit (from administration area three). The forces from these reserves and villages occupied positions around the villages of Panuslu, Girdekan and Hijalan, and occupied the Okhchu-Shabadak mountains at night. After four days of exhausting battles the Muslim volunteers assembled in the house of Molla Hasan Efendi to discuss whether to continue the battle, or withdraw. Many views were expressed by various people. Even the women behind the curtain, which divided them from the men in the room, said some words which encouraged the men and challenged them to continue the battle. There were two opinions: either to continue the battle, or to withdraw. Finally, Molla Hasan Efendi, who was the Imam* of the village and also a Sayyid, a descendant of the martyrs of Islam, delivered a speech, which we adapt to our own style for the understanding of readers:

"Brothers! The fascinating light of the moon has illuminated the tops of the mountains surrounding us on all four sides. The dark

* Spiritual person, leading public worship in the mosque.

shapes trembling below in the woods are the banners of the Armenians. Look at them closely! The walls which surround us and which aim their rifles at us are the Armenian detachments, the brutes of Hayastan (Armenia). My sons, it is the same for us whether we withdraw, or attack the enemy. In both cases it is obvious that we shall become martyrs. There is not a shred of mercy in the hearts of the Armenians for our children and women. Tomorrow morning the Armenians will begin the attack. But you are not in a position to attack the enemy, you remain on the defensive. Do not leave your positions until the last breath.

When you feel that defeat is near, do not leave your positions all at once, otherwise, the enemy will pursue you. You will suffer great losses. You must leave some strong and skilful young men in the rear, as dumdars,[38] the rest will take the women and children to the woods, to the foot of the mountains and find shelter there."

When Molla Hasan Efendi's speech reached this point, heart-rending wails and cries arose from the women and men there. Molla Hasan Efendi continued his speech:

"Brothers! To cry with the women, to join them in their elegies will do no good. It can only discourage a man, weaken his spiritual power, tie his hands and arms before the enemy and lead to lethargy. Now take your rifles and other weapons, repair, clean and make them ready for battle". Then he recited the opening chapter (Al Fatihah)* of the Holy Koran and resumed reading the holy book.

After his speech, the men present counted their rifles. There were several Berdanka rifles and a few hundred cartridges left. The rest of the rifles were not fit for use after being fired continuously for four days. When the people saw that their supplies were not sufficient to continue the war, they took the women and children and

---

[38] The late Molla Hasan Efendi used many words in his speech worthy of praise. The word dumdar probably means rearguard, used as a term by the military in many wars. Dumdars were used when the army retreated in order to delay the march of the enemy and to allow their own army to retreat without leaving trophies for the enemy. When an army retreats and finds a favourable position, the dumdars suddenly retreat and prevent the enemy from pursuing.

* Funeral prayers.

walked towards Saggarsu, which stood in the direction opposite to Mecca. They found shelter behind the mountains around Saggarsu. The cries of the women echoed in the Armenian shelters and in their trenches on top of the rocks. Molla Hasan Efendi also found shelter there with his family. Only people greedy for property, the disabled, blind women and old people unable to move, remained in the village. At dawn the Armenians attacked the village, murdered everybody there and looted the village. The corpses of the slaughtered lay in heaps.

The painful events of Saggarsu

At dawn a group of men shouting "Ali, Ali"[39] approached Saggarsu, where the Muslims had found shelter. The Muslims thought that they were Muslim troops coming to help them and left the shelter to meet them, crying with joy. But they were Armenians; as soon as they reached the Muslims, they began to cut and slaughter them. At the same time slaughter was also being carried out in four other Muslim villages. The inhabitants of these villages found sanctuary in Ordubad and they talked about the tragedy which had befallen the Muslims in Saggarsu. When everybody had been killed, or had escaped, Molla Hasan Efendi, with several women and with a Holy Koran in his hand, came out of the shelter to meet the Armenians, hoping that they would pardon them for the sake of the Holy Koran. But these irreligious men, who perhaps disregarded not only the Holy Koran, but also the Bible, showed no mercy to anyone and savagely killed them all. Several Korans and other holy books were taken from Molla Hasan Efendi, bayonetted and burned like torches. No one in the world had ever acted as cruelly as the Armenians up to that time. The Muslim women, men and children, cold and hungry, who had escaped, roamed like sick sheep for several days, in shabby clothes or naked, before reaching Ordubad and the villages close to it. The people of Ordubad were very hospitable and, as they had suffered from such misfortunes before, displayed great care for these unfortunate people.

---

[39] Imam Ali is meant; when people cry for help, they call to him

The fate of the victims of the Okchu-Shabadak tragedy in Ordubad

When the victims of the Okhchu-Shabadak tragedy arrived in Ordubad, crying and in a very poor state, it shocked and grieved the residents of Ordubad very much. They provided the refugees with rooms and spaces to rest and stay. First they dealt with the wounded, finding surgeons and medicine to treat them. The refugees were supplied with goods and other necessities of life and home; they tried to find rest and comfort. Then about one hundred letters and telegrams were sent to the government on their behalf. This small town, endowed by God with wealth and food, supplied the refugees with all the necessities of life within a day, then organised to rescue the Muslims who had remained in the mountains, to find the wounded and do what was necessary for them, to take them to the town and to bury the dead. They organized a detachment with medicine and doctors to treat and carry the wounded, to bury the corpses, to find cloth for shrouds and for tents. After all these preparations, the detachment started out for the mountains on the evening of 16 August 1906.

The first visit of the detachment from Ordubad to Gapan Gorge

The detachment from Ordubad to the battle-field in Okhchu-Shabadak assembled in the Muslim village of Nugadi at 8 o'clock on 16 August and remained there until the arrival of all the equipment necessary for the journey from Ordubad. By 12 o'clock everything had arrived; it was given to a special transport detachment to be taken to a high mountain called Ayi Changili. At 2 o'clock the supplies and the guards, as well as the detachment, reached Nugadi and stopped to rest for a while. Then they posted rear guards and at 8 o'clock moved off. On 17 August 1906, at 4 o'clock in the afternoon, the detachment reached Saggarsu. The vanguard, sent by cart, had already built a tent and heated it inside. This pleased the main detachment which arrived later. Too impatient to wait any longer, they began to cover the area and look for traces of the slaughter. It was an hour and a half before dusk; rain and sleet were pouring down, a strong wind was pulling the tent pegs out of the ground.[40]

A mixture of rain and snow was raging and the wind hurled snow at their faces like pellets from a hunter's gun.

The weather was so awful that it was impossible to walk or even to stand on one spot. The strong winds of the Gapan Gorge sounded like cannons on the mountain peaks of Shabadak, the drifts of snow were growing by the minute. The weather changed for better or worse several times within half an hour. Many people were injured between Ordubad and the mountains; they were bandaged and sent to the town.

Despite the rain and snow, they decided to take some guides and explore the surroundings. In the distance they saw a pool of blood near Saggarsu and started in that direction. The surface of the pool was frozen, but blood was leaking in drops from the stones. This surprised and astonished the search party. They informed the main detachment in the tent. The corpses of 62 women and children had been piled up on top of each other. The sight made everybody cry. After a while they heard a faint whimper from among the women's bodies. After a careful search, they found that there was a woman, wounded in both legs, who was hovering between life and death and producing the whimper. The poor woman was taken to the tent. After some time she gained consciousness and amid her tears she said the following:

"We were with Molla Hasan Efendi. The Armenians stabbed him with daggers. We ran and sheltered behind a rock. When they had finished with Molla Hasan Efendi, the Armenians rushed after us and slaughtered everybody there. Half of my body was unhidden. There were so many children and women among the rocks that I could not hide myself completely and so several Armenians

---

[40] This tragedy has not been related by reporters orally or in written form before. It has been examined with a truthful eye and entered into history. Much time is needed to write about the events of Okhchu-Shabadak, it will make history if it is all put onto paper. However, we must be content for now only with the information below.

reached out and cut my legs which were protruding from the rocks. At that moment an Armenian, apparently one of their commanders, or elders, stopped them from killing me and said:

"We are waging a war against the Muslims in the Caucasus. Not against the Sunnis, but the Shiites. The misfortunes afflicting you are due to the actions of the Sultan of Ottoman against the Armenians in Turkey. All this slaughter is because of the Ottomans, you must know it! All the tortures you suffer will not equal those suffered by Armenian women in Sasun, Zeytun and Van and inflicted with the support of the government. Armenian women have been captured and converted to Islam. What we are doing is not half of the revenge to be taken for them".

The poor woman's wounds were very serious, she was not sent to the town, but to the Muslim village of Pezmeri. The night was spent in Saggarsu. An eye witness continued to describe events:

"On 18 August, after the dawn prayer, we went to the forest where people were thought to have found refuge. After some time we found the bodies of a young woman of about 25 and of a young man, they seemed to be wife and husband. They had been stabbed together. Then we reached the spot where Molla Hasan Efendi had been slaughtered. His corpse, prayer accessories and other holy items had been burnt. A little to the north of that spot we saw a piece of pileless carpet which covered the bodies of 15 children, their throats had been cut and the bodies had been laid on top of each other. The wind had piled snow over them. The sight made everybody cry. The snow was red with the blood of women and children and resembled a field of tulips in spring. The ground was frozen and hard to dig. We covered the corpses with tree branches and leaves. Then we descended from Saggarsu towards the village of Purdavud. First we went to the Sanctuary of Sultan Davud, brother of Imam Rza. Nothing remained of the sanctuary except its bare dome. Everything inside had been burned. According to the guide's story, the Armenians had burned the Holy Korans and thrown them out of the window one by one. The Armenians, who claim to teach culture to the Europeans, had done other things, too. Molla Hasan

Efendi had had a picture of the outstanding men of the world sent to him as a gift in 1901. Also in the picture were portraits of Prophet Muhammad (Hail to Him) and Omar (May God be his guardian). They had burned the picture only because of Muhammad and Omar. In short, after the visit to the sanctuary we could not tolerate the cold of Purdavud and went to the village of Okhchu. I think that the painful scenes we saw there are beyond any description, no one could put them all down onto paper.

Near the village we saw numerous animal corpses on the ground, piled up on top of each other. There were also animals not yet dead, but trembling in their death agony, the bowels of one cow had fallen out. It all made one go crazy. It recalled the battle of Macedonia and the battle near Liaoyang.[41] The human corpses piled together formed high hills like in those battles. The sight was terrible and maddening. Or it was like the battle of Velistan between Turkey and Greece. The Greek corpses piled in heaps on the battlefield caught the eye at once. On one side, at the foot of the mountain, there were slaughtered infants, like cradles with red swaddling bands across the stones and the rock stained with blood.

On the other side, a house was still smoking. We went there and found a young man slaughtered. Close to his head there was the body of an old woman cut into pieces with a dagger. The guides said that the young man had been wounded in the battle, but her mother had not left him and remained behind, so she had been stabbed to death close to her son. When we reached the village of Okchu, the Armenians were carrying away the corpses of their dead to the villages of Panuslu and Girdekan.

The reason the Armenians had not carried away the corpses of their dead soldiers before then was the severe cold. We were informed that there were still two Armenian corpses on the river bank.

One of the bodies was of a young man about 25-30, the other about 45-50 years old. We searched their clothes. On one of them was a piece of bloodstained paper, on the other a package of papers

---

[41] Battle near Liaoyang - The Russian-Japanese war of 1904, in which the Russian army was defeated.

without envelopes. The heading on one of the papers was in Russian. It was to be delivered to Stepan Saakyans, a member of the Dashnaksutyun Party, by Vachisyans in the village of Mehri. In translation, the paper said:

"My dear son! Your younger brother also joined the Dashnaksutyun Party recently and was sent out of the country. Do not spare your efforts one minute for the sake of the nation! Each of your swords fighting for the nation will become a bunch of flowers placed on the graves of the fighters who died in Turkey for Armenia. Your mother was a little ill. The news that you are well (blood had made the rest of the line illegible. Then it continued)... Of course, everything will be arranged for the 25th of this month. Your sister Oskuyey gave birth to twin sons. They must also be considered two soldiers for the sake of our nation".

The letter was written in the province of Zeytun of Turkey and signed by T.G.Azizyan.

The second letter was from the village of Sardov in the province of Garadagh in Iran. It was for Vartanyans Karapet in Hadrut. Here are its contents:

"This letter is written to Karapet Vartayans by his beloved Varvara. Today Nerses came from Tabriz.

Muhammad Ali Mirza[*] has got the shah's decree in which he expresses his love for the Armenians. These days the atmosphere in Iran is very mild and beneficial for the Armenians.

Nerses says that the Muslims of Iran remain neutral in the affairs of the Muslims in the Caucasus. It is clear that the khans of Iran are not living with the illusions of the past. We have enough food at home. Do not worry about us. It would be better if you returned before the cold begins! Do not go in the direction of Shusha.

Many people from our neighbouring villages have been killed in Shusha......Signed: Varvara".

---

[*] Muhammad Ali Mirza, Prince, later Shah of Iran (1907-1909).

After the village of Okhchu, we passed through the villages of Shabadak and Atgiz. The latter had suffered the greatest losses. Bodies were buried only under leaves and twigs. The Armenians did not do anything to us."

The property lost in the village was worth one million roubles. The battles in this village began on 9 August and finished on 16 August 1906. The Muslims lost about 200 men, women and children killed. As there was not an exact list of the population, it was impossible to know the exact number of dead. The battles in Zengezur began in early June and continued till the end of August. We have spoken about all of them, one after another. Those villages were the following:

Khalaj, Karkhana, Gatar, Injevar, Chollu, Yemezli, Saldashli, Mollalar, Batuman, Okchu, Shabadak, Atgiz, Purdavud, Zurum, Guman, Iyilli, Senali, Minenevur, Ferjan, Galaboynu, Esebli and Bugachig. All these Muslim villages have been looted by the Armenians.

The second visit of the people of Ordubad to Okhchu-Shabadak and news of the war

As the victims of the Okchu-Shabadak tragedy had scattered to the villages in the province and to Ordubad, people were greatly excited and agitated. The people of Ordubad sent about 100 telegrams to the governors general of both provinces and delivered to them news of the slaughter of the Muslim population. After so many telegrams a mounted dragoon company arrived, to be at the disposal of the governor general. By order of the latter, the residents of the above-mentioned villages were taken back to their own villages, accompanied by the military. They had hardly reached Saggarsu, when the Armenians fired several shots and killed two Muslims in the presence of the military.

The officers of the dragoon company sent telegrams to their chiefs; the texts have been published in all the Caucasian newspapers. In this way, when the people arrived in their native villages, openly or secretly, they were met by Armenians who fired at them, and they were forced to turn back. As we have already mentioned, when the Armenians occupied Okhchu-Shabadak, they received orders not to let the Muslims return there again. This was their policy. Further, soldiers exhausted by the fighting had been sent home and replaced by new ones, because they were sure that there would be new battles to re-take Okchu-Shabadak. The Armenians had mainly been afraid of the beys of Javanshir and Sultanov. But they did not display any love for their nation or religion. Sure of their impunity, the Armenians were destroying the houses in Okhchu, reaping the fields and taking the corn to the nearby Armenian villages.

As all the villages nearby had been captured by the Armenians, the people of Okhchu, without support and unprotected, had streamed into Ordubad; their miserable state was painful and heartbreaking. The refugees needed warm rooms in the town, especially as winter was approaching. Besides, because of the fighting, communications with Karabagh had been broken and trade in the town and among the population was not at a satisfactory level. There was not enough food to supply the starving people who had been added to the regular inhabitants of the town. Further, the refugees were used to living in mountainous areas where wood for fires was abundant, but in the town coal was very expensive, it was a problem to supply them with warmth and convenience in winter. The residents of Okhchu were cattle-breeders, but there were not sufficient stables and pens in the town to keep the cattle and flocks of sheep, or the fodder to feed the animals in winter; they were sure to starve to death. For all these reasons, some of the refugees were very keen to return to their destroyed villages and they constantly begged the townsfolk to let them go. Meanwhile, the townsfolk's love for the refugees grew day by day, they shared their flats and rooms with them. But we should also say that the love of the Okhchu villagers for their native home also grew from day to day.

Different opinions emerged in the town and province concerning the refugees' desire to return home and it was decided to call a council. After several discussions it was decided to return the refugees to their homes by all means necessary. After numerous consultations, the people of Okhchu and other villages were asked to make preparations for the return, because some of them had driven their cattle and sheep away while escaping. On the other hand, the desire of the Armenian intelligence associations to permanently occupy the villages was also growing. This lust and thirst of the Armenians created obstacles to the projected return to Okhchu, although the Muslims' desire to return home was a desire blessed by God.

Despite all the above, the people of Ordubad and of the province would not change their minds and were preparing to achieve their aim. At first they wanted to do it officially through the government but, as the troubles raged in Zengezur, and these events coincided with the most critical moments in the Russian revolution, the government was not strong enough to punish and contain the Armenians. Thus the Muslim population had to rely on their own courage and strength. The residents of Ordubad took on the obligation to punish the Armenians and began to make preparations to suppress the Armenians of Panuslu and Girdekan.

*Mobilization of the army to be sent to the battlefield of Panuslu and Girdekan, or the plan of campaign**

If a tribe or nation is compelled to wage war, first of all it develops a plan of campaign, starting with the geographical location of the battlefield. Then it tries to mobilize sufficient military forces for the capture of the battlefield and for the dispatch of its forces to that spot. When these two decisions are made, it then thinks about where to raise the military force and where and when to assemble it. Military supplies and weapons are transported to the soldiers' assembly point, or to friendly villages close to the battlefield, and their security is arranged.

According to plan, battlefield supplies from Ordubad were

---

* see map on page 170.

transported to nearby Muslim villages four days before the beginning of the battle, in order to be delivered to Saggarsu in time. On 15 September 1906, the soldiers got the order to move and assemble in Saggarsu. At about 12 o'clock they were ready at the top of Saggarsu. On that day organizational work was done until evening and scouts were sent to reconnoitre the surrounding area. By the evening there were already 800 soldiers with modern rifles, about one thousand armed residents of Okhchu-Shabadak and volunteers who had come under arms of their own free will. The number of soldiers soon grew to 1800. On 15 September, at 7 o'clock in the evening, the people, together with the military, held a council in Saggarsu. All the forces assembled there were united under a single command; three commanders were also appointed from existing forces. Each of them was given regular soldiers. The commander-in-chief developed all the necessary plans and ordered the detachment commanders to fulfil them strictly.

Each of the three commanders also appointed commanders of groups consisting of ten soldiers and informed the commander-in-chief. At 9pm, the first of the three detachments sent out scouts, then marched from Saggarsu, crossed the top of the mountain near the village of Shabadak and passed through the destroyed village of Atgiz and the foot of the mountains, reaching the lower part of the village of Girdekan. An hour before dawn they got the order to begin the battle. 50 mounted fighters were also sent to support them as a reserve. At 10pm the second detachment was ordered to start from Saggarsu, pass through the village of Panuslu by the Okhchu road, build fortifications and attack the enemy an hour before dawn. A special communications group was set up from the cavalry to control the actions of the detachments. The third detachment was ordered to march at 12 midnight to occupy the Lej and Feshtin mountain passes and to prevent Armenians from the village of Mehri and other Armenian villages from helping their compatriots and, if necessary, to join the battle. Another 500 volunteers were kept in reserve.

After the the three detachments had set off, the commander-in-chief moved from Saggarsu, which was the general headquarters, and organized a corps in Shabadak under the command of one experienced soldier. It consisted of 150 mounted fighters and 200 infantry. Another 50 regular soldiers were selected to ensure the delivery of information between the fighting detachments and 200 volunteers from the residents of Okhchu and Shabadak were detailed to ensure the supply of food and ammunition to the front. After allocating the necessary tasks, the commander-in-chief returned to headquarters in Saggarsu. An order to assist the detachments in Girdekan and Panuslu reached the commander of the Shabadak detachment at 3 o'clock. Twenty five mounted soldiers were ordered to ensure the delivery of military information between the detachments and headquarters. The detachments reached their destination at about 3 o'clock and occupied the most suitable positions on hilltops and mountain peaks; they built fortifications and sent scouts to collect information from the villages of Panuslu and Girdekan. One hour before dawn the Muslims started the battle.

16 September 1906

One hour before dawn, the first detachment got the order from the commander-in-chief to open fire on the village of Panuslu. Several minutes later the second detachment, which was close to Panuslu, joined the battle. At that point the Armenians had significant military forces in the two villages. When the firing began, they occupied their shelters and trenches and began to reply to the Muslims. While the Muslims were sounding trumpets and other wind instruments, the Armenian villages were wrapped in silence, as if there was nobody in the villages, except for the unending sound of firearms shooting from the trenches. Thus, the battle continued for four hours and then an Armenian detachment attempted to cut communications between the Muslim fighters located in Girdekan and Panuslu, but they were defeated by a reserve detachment kept in Atgiz. The Armenians lost 80 soldiers killed in the battle, which continued for five hours.

The Muslim command was aware of the enemy's forces. The

Armenians ordered their reserves to join the battle. At 10 o'clock a bloody fight began. The Muslim fighters left their shelters and attacked the Armenian positions. The Armenians retreated to the village, took shelter in the church and houses, but continued to battle fiercely. The Muslim soldiers gradually approached the village. They were ordered not to fire at the church. It was surrounded. In the battle, which continued until 12 o'clock, the Armenians were defeated, the Muslim villages were liberated. At one o'clock, scouts from the first Muslim detachment reported the movement of government troops, 500 in number. When the news arrived, the first detachment was signalled by trumpet to retreat and join the second detachment. The snipers of the first and second detachments set several of the village houses on fire. Headquarters sent an order to the detachment commanders to call the snipers back.

When news came from the detachment defending Teshtikh that the chief of police of Zengezur province was coming with 500 Cossacks, the two villages were on the verge of complete destruction. Headquarters ordered the detachments to retreat and return to Saggarsu, where headquarters was located. After one hour the government troops entered the village from both sides. This was observed from headquarters through binoculars. At dawn on 17 August, the Muslims left Saggarsu and returned home. As the government troops had arrived, the residents of Okhchu and Shabadak returned and settled in their destroyed villages.

17 September 1906

Residents of Okchu return home

After being defeated on 16 August 1906, the Armenians of Panuslu and Girdekan completely relinquished their previous claims and insatiability, as well as their habit of troubling the Muslims. The government also awoke from its slumber and sent Cossacks and troops to those parts of the country to ensure order and security. The population breathed with some relief. After the failure of their policy, the Armenian intelligence associations also abandoned their efforts to occupy the villages of Okchu and Shabadak. Their defeat at the battle of Panuslu-Girdekan hung like a stone round their necks. Thus the residents of the villages of Okhchu and Shabadak returned home. As many houses had been destroyed, there were cases of two or three families sharing a house and living on hand-outs and charity which came from the neighbouring villages. The inhabitants of Ordubad and the province displayed great courage and love for their compatriots; they adorned our history with pages written in gold and cherished it. May God make them happy in both worlds. Amen!

INDEX

Abaran............................53, 173, 174
Abbas bey...83
Abbas Hasan oglu.............................134
Abbasgulu Hasankhan oglu..............113
Abil bey, policeman..........................128
Adamov.......................................96, 98
Adamov's shop....................................37
Afshar, village..........................65, 75, 77
Agamalov............................34, 36, 37
Agarak, village..................................177
Agarza; Agarza, Babayev.......25, 26, 28
Agayev Ahmed bey...................16, 146,
......150, 152, 154, 155, 156, 158
Agbulag, village......................69, 70, 76
Agchal, street....................................138
Agdam....................................75, 174, 175
Agdam road..67
Agdere, village..................................124
Agoglan monastery.............................58
Agulis, village...........................174, 175
Aguz..174
Ahmed Karbalayi Gasim oglu............57
Ahmedli, village..................................75
Akhladina, village.............................145
Akhullu, village............................69, 76
Akhund Muhammad Ali Mirza Huseyn..52
Akhundov Mirza...............................139
Akim Isayevich...................................28
Akopov Nikolay................................101
Alavar.......................................137, 138
Alayiz Mountains................................53
Alexandropol.............51, 53, 173, 174
Alftan, General...........................90, 133
Ali Alinagi oglu................................131
Ali ibn Abu Talib................................71
Ali Mirza, Muhammad.....................184
Aliabad..34
Aliagali, village........................110, 114
Alibeyli, village.......................142, 145

Alibeyov; Alibeyov I. 126, 127
Alikhanov-Avarski, General Maksud..42
Alisevskiy...101
Aliyev Agakishi..................................28
Aliyev's house..................................100
Alps..148
America..21
Amilov..27
Amir Aslan Ali Pasha oglu...............134
Amospirov Vaso...............................134
Amrah Hasan oglu............................127
Anapur, river................................53, 55
Anatolia..21
Andriyans................................113, 132
Angil, Nakhchivan district chief.......19,
......................................20, 37, 38, 39
Ani..22
Antonov..96
'Araj' newspaper..............................161
Arakelyan..................................146, 160
Aram...19, 172
Aramyans, Mirza................................29
Ardagan..22
Aresh district......................................20
Armenia...................................22, 85, 184
Armenian Archimandrite............85, 130
Armenian Bazaar........................82, 138
Armenian charity organization of
    Mikhailov....................................96
Armenian commanders..........47, 63, 65
Armenian Committee.......................109
Armenian detachments..............51, 54,
......................130, 141, 142, 178, 189
Arsenov Arsen..................................144
Artemyans, Mikhail............................28
Artsruni...22, 23
Arutyunov Samson...........146, 157, 160
Arish, village.................................70, 74
Arzumanov family.............................28

INDEX

Asad..112
Asadazur, village..............................177
Ashot............................58, 63, 65, 175
Ashurbey, street................................100
Asker khan.......................................118
Askerkhan, Gochag..........................115
Askerkhanov Hasanali bey..........64, 65
Askeran..90
Askeran road......................................91
Askerkhan, Gochag..........................115
Askipara, village..............141, 142, 145
Aslanovs' house............................29, 30
Astamal, village................................172
Atabeyov..82
Atali, village.....................................144
Atans...131
Atgiz, village....................185, 188, 189
Athens..112
Avakov's house..................................96
Avetisov Avetis........................127, 154
Avetisov Stepan.................................28
Avshar, village...................................76
Avsharov..99
Ayi Changili, mountain....................180
Ayibli, village...................................142
Ayrapet..51
Ayrapetyans' shops............................27
Ayrim, village..................................142
Azad, village....................................135
Azaryans Melik................................168
Azerbaijan.................................22, 112
Azizyan T.G. 184
Babajanov..28
Babayev Abdulali...............................31
Bagaburj, village..............................177
Baganis, village................................142
Baganis-Ayrim, village....................142
Bagirov Ahmed................................101
Bagirov garden (now Azim Azimzade
    Square)..100
Bagirov's house..................................97
Bagrat..19
Bahadurov..................................22, 150
Bahmanli, village...............18, 134, 135

Bahrvar, village................................177
Bakhtiyev Agadadash........................99
Baku..............................16, 18, 19, 20, 21,
....23,25, 26, 27, 29, 30, 31, 33, 41,45,
....51, 66, 81, 95, 97, 98, 101, 102, 146
Baku police................................98, 102
Balakahni oil fields....................27, 101
Balakhani....................................31, 101
Balakhanskaya, street (now Fizuli Street)
    ....99, 100, 101, 102
Balyupchi, village............................145
Barabatum, village..................164, 167,
    ....168, 169, 177
Baranovsky V.P. 34, 36, 85
Bashir...144
Bashkeni, village................................52
Batumi.................................103, 107, 108
Batuman, village..............................185
Bauver, General...............................109
Bayram Meshedi Muhammadali oglu
    ....127, 135
Bayramzade Ali Haji.........................34
Bazarnaya, street (now Azerbaijan
    Avenue)....................................27, 100
Bedo...19
Berdan; Berdanka, rifle..............98, 178
Berlin...21
Berlin Congress.................................21
Beyler bey...63
Birjevaya street (now U. Hajibeyov
    Street)..99
Bizhans..22
Bolshaya Morskaya street (now Bulbul
    Avenue)....................................28, 100
Boulevard....................................29, 46
Boyuk Koloniya Street....................135
Bugachig, village.............................185
Bukh, village....................................177
Caucasians..................................59, 107
Caucasus..................14, 15, 16, 18, 19,
....20, 21, 22, 23, 26, 33, 50, 79, 80, 90,
....103, 106, 107, 113, 119, 120, 126,
....136, 138, 145, 146, 147, 148, 149,
..152, 154, 155, 158, 161, 162, 182,184

INDEX

Chadrovaya Street (now M.M. Aliyev Street)..26
Chakhmagli, village................141, 142
Chanakchi, village..............................63
Changchi...58
Chardagli, village............................142
Chartaz, village.....................58, 62, 63
Chartazly Bakhshi, Bakhshi...............58
Chayli, village............................116, 118
Chekedek, village..............,......164, 177
Chemen, village................................177
Chemenli, village................................69
Chernits, Justice of the Peace...........132
Cheshmebasar, village.......................38
Chikhaduz, village..............................63
Chin, village......................................177
Chiragli, village..110, 116,118, 119,120
Chiraguz, village.................................67
Chit, village......................................177
Chollu, village..................................185
Cossacks.........20, 27, 38, 39, 40, 81, 92,
............94, 97, 114, 116, 119, 120, 128,
........134, 142, 143, 145, 167 169, 190,
Crete, island.....................................145

Dadashov's house............................100
Dagestan...153
Dagestan, regiment.................30, 97, 98
Daghbasar villages...........................124
Damagirmez, village..........................52
Dashnak committee...........114, 115, 132
Dashnaks......................42, 63, 93, 115,
.................................121, 128, 134, 135
Dashnaksutyun ("Union"), Armenian
 Nationalist Party............18, 19, 21, 22,
  27, 45, 57, 58, 61, 63, 111, 112, 116,
  118, 121, 124, 126, 159, 160, 163,
  ....165, 184
Dashnov, village..............................166
Davud Sultan....................................182
Davydov....................................74, 76
Deli Ali..158
Demgurt, village..............................174
Demirchiler, village...........................141
Demirli, village................110, 116, 120

Derebagin...134
Dilagarda, village...............................58
Dilijan..143
Dirnis, village..................................174
Divanali...................................58, 62, 76
Dolanlar, village..........................74, 76
Dolkhanov...82
Dovletov's house...............................99
Dubrovin..98
Dudukchu, village........................68, 76
Duma Square (now Youth Square)..101
Durniyans Arshak...............................28

Echmiadzin............................22, 53, 60
Eizbash......................................97, 102
England......................................21, 160
Enkirsek, village.................................55
Esebli, village..................................185
Europe......................................148, 153
Fadeyev S.A. 102
Farahli, village.................................142
Farid Abdul Zeynal oglu..................101
Ferjan, village..................................185
Feshtin..188
Filiposyans brothers.........................100
Firdausi..92
First Capitan street..........................100
Firuza...165
Fleisher......................................89, 133
Fligbel..115
France.......................107, 160, 162
Frelikh...90
Fuladov Khosrov bey........................82

Gapan Gorge....165, 173, 174, 180, 181
Gajar, village........57, 58, 61, 63, 64, 65
Galaboynu, village...........................185
Galadibi..51
Gamsaragan..............126, 127, 128, 135
Ganja......................18, 19, 21, 23, 109,
   126, 127, 130, 133, 134, 146, 148
Ganja province, officially Elizavetpol
 province..57, 78, 89, 90, 109, 110, 119, 173
Ganja(Elizavetpol) district.........21, 126
Ganja, river......................................130
Gapanlinsky Abil bey..............127, 131

INDEX

Gara..82
Gara Mahmud, firelock....................112
Garabeyov, Doctor Gara bey.....146, 152
Garabulag bazaar...............................66
Garachay gardens, Irevan...................42
Garachemen, village........................165
Garadagh................................172, 184
Garadaghli, village.............................76
Garagoyunlu....................................144
Garakhanyan.....................................29
Garapetov Arshak Aziz oglu............139
Garpiz Square...........................138, 139
Gart...51
Gasim Boyukkishi oglu...................135
Gasimzade Molla Abdurrahim...........61
Gatar.........................164, 165, 166, 167,
......168, 169, 172, 174, 175, 177, 185
Gate of Irevan...................................82
Gazakh..............19, 133, 135, 141, 142,
....143, 144, 145
Gazi of Irevan.................42, 46, 56, 73
Geneva..19
Georgian brothers........................60, 80
Georgian, Georgians.......39, 60, 80, 96,
................99, 129, 132, 139, 162, 163
Geray, Sultan of the Crimea............146
Gezlek, village..................................74
Gimnazicheskaya street (now Tolstoy
Street)...100
Girchivan, village............................177
Girdekan, village.............175, 177, 183,
...................................187, 188, 189, 190
Girkhbulag............................49, 50, 53
Gishlag, village.................................74
Gizilhajili, village.....................141, 142
Gnchak ("Bell"), Armenian Nationalist
Party..19, 132
Gojayev Haji Samed.......................131
Goloshapov, Chief of Shusha district
..................20, 77, 89, 90, 91, 92, 93,
....94, 109, 133
Golovinskiy Avenue........................138
Gorus district....................................91
Gosha Chinar..............................18, 134

Goshabulag, village...........................55
Gozechik, village.........................49, 51
Grisha..66
Grisha, hatter...................................134
Guba meydani (square) (now Fizuli
Square)..102
Guberniskaya Street (now Nizami
Street).......................................27, 29
Gudsi-Sharif (Jerusalem).............
Gulluje, village............................51, 52
Gultepe, village.................................34
Guman, village................................185
Gurasan, village...............................177
Gurban bayramy..............................141
Gygyn valley..........................

Hadrut.......................................74, 184
Hagbeli, village................................142
Haji Naghi Agahuseyn oglu.............131
Haji Efendi.....................................104
Haji Fatali Aghali oglu......................31
Haji Huseyn.....................................52
Haji Nasir Haji Nagi oglu.................38
Hajigarvend, village.........110, 113, 115,
....118, 119, 120
Hajiyev Karbalayi Israfil............146, 153,
....156, 160
Hajiyev brothers................................31
Hajjali, village.................................142
Hamazasp...................19, 114, 124, 125
Hasan bey Fatalibeyov, police..128, 131
Hasan Meshedi, son of Mammadgulu
bey..39
Hasangaya, village....................110, 123
Hasanov, police...............................100
Hashimov Aga Sultanali....................31
Hayastan........................85, 173, 178
Heyat ("Life"), newspaper.......102, 103
Heydar aga..............................107, 108
Heyvali, village................................121
Hijalan, village........................176, 177
Hummet bey Pasha bey oglu............113
Huseyn ibn Ali Aleyhussalam............71
Huseyngulu Karbalayi Abdulla oglu.....28
Huseyngulu Mahmudov....................28

INDEX

Huseynzade Hummet bey....................49
Ibrahimov Haji Najafgulu...................31
Icheri Sheher..97
Ilanchalan, village...............................53
Iman Hasankhan oglu........................113
Imaret Garvand, village............110, 123
Injevar, village.............................166, 185
Inozemsev, Captain.............................98
Iran...........................21, 22, 23, 27, 79,
....82, 95, 108, 184
Irevan..................23, 33, 34, 36, 39, 40,
........41, 42, 45, 46, 47, 48, 49, 52, 53,
.... 105, 106, 107, 110, 111, 146,
...............148, 158, 164, 173, 174, 175
Irevan province.....................41, 47, 103
Irevanski Abbasgulu khan..................46
Irevan-Zengezur, road......................174
Irgu, village...55
Irmashli, village..................................142
Irshad ("To put the truth in place"), newspaper....................16, 57, 110, 119
Isayevich, Colonel.............................133
Ishkhanov Agabey 19, 63, 65, 66, 69
Ismayil..120, 121
Ismayil bey..114
Ismayilbeyli, village..........................110
Ispandaryan......................................156
Israfil bey..141
Israfil, Archangel..............................176
Istanbul..22, 79
Itgiranlar, village...............................174
Iyilli, village.......................................185

Jabbar Huseyn oglu..........................134
Jabrail.......................19, 20, 57, 61, 62,
...................................66, 67, 77, 90, 164
Jabrail Jafargulu oglu..........................69
Jabrail-Karyagin district...............67, 76
Jafar Mirbaba oglu............................101
Jafarli, village....................................142
Jafarov Meshedi Hanifa......................28
Jafarzade Mir Muhammad Kerim aga Mir, Gazi...101
Jahanbakhshbey.................................51
Jahri, village........33, 34, 37, 39, 40, 174

Jalalov, Aram bey Hasan...................121
Jalil, police...166
Jamal bey...165
Javad district...
Javanshir.........19, 20, 90, 109, 110, 112,
.......115, 117, 118, 119, 122, 150, 164
Javanshir Ahmed bey........................119
Javanshir beys..........155, 116, 118, 119,
...................................122, 123, 125, 186
Javanshir district..............110, 111, 113,
....115, 125, 148
Javanshir, clan...................................113
Javanshir Javad aga..........................114
Jerusalem...22

Kakhlilar, village...............................110
Kalantar.........................146, 147, 149,
....150, 151, 152, 157
Kamal...52
Karabagh........23, 89, 90, 111, 114, 186
Karabagh Khanate....................113, 119
Karantinnaya, street (now Hazi Aslanov Street)...100
Karavat, village.................................177
Karbala..71
Karbalayi Ali Baltachi oglu.............128
Karbalayi Faraj Hasan oglu.............134
Karbalayi Muhammad Ibrahim oglu....127
Karbalayi Novruz Muhammad oglu....144
Karkhana, village.............165, 166, 185
Karlur, village...................................177
Kars...22, 23
Kars sanjak..23
Karvansara................................142, 143
Karyagin..........................20, 57, 66, 67
Kaspi Street (now R. Behbudov Street)
....100
Kaspiy, newspaper.....................18, 135
Kaspiy, printing house.......................16
Kazakh..21
Kazimli..142
Kazimoglu Novruz.................49, 50, 51
Kazizade Muhammad Ali Mirza Abdul Huseyn...184
Kelagi, village...................................174

196

INDEX

Kelledag, village......................169, 171
Kengerli Muhammadgulu bey...103-108
Khachatur..36
Khachin Gorge....................109, 123, 124
Khachin, river.................................110
Khalaj, village..................166, 169, 185
Khalatovs..37
Khalfali, quarter...............................83
Khan, Jafargulu................................36
Khanavenk, river.........................53, 54
Khandemirov theatre........................85
Khankendi, village...........................93
Khanlilar, village............................174
Kharpukh...137
Khasmamedov Aliakber bey...........146
Khasmammadov Ali Asker.............132
Khatisov..................146, 154, 159, 160
Khazaz, mountain..................63, 64, 65
Kheyrimli, village...........................142
Khirmanjig, village..........70, 71, 72, 76
Khojayev...132
Khoshandam, village...................75, 76
Khotanan, village...........................177
Khunbabat yuvasi (nest)...................74
Kichikkend, village..........................55
Kinigar, priest.................................144
Kocharli, quarter..........................83, 92
Kohnegishlag, village.....................142
Kolanlar, villages............................110
Kolanli, village..................109, 117, 127
Kolyubakinskaya Street
 (now N. Rafibeyli Street)..............102
Konapay, village.............................110
Koran....49, 51, 55, 56, 144, 178, 179, 182
Korsakov...27
Kotuklu, village.................................55
Krasilnikovs......................................26
Krasnavodskaya Street
 (now Samed Vurgun street)........28, 97
Krylov, Cossack commander.....20, 38, 39
Kubinka...25
Kudikov's house................................98
Kudkum, village..............................177
Kurd Mahmud, village......................74

Kurds......................................45, 51, 149
Kursininskaya street.......................138
Kuzminsky, Lt Colonel.....................28
Labinsky regiment..............................97
Lahij..112
Laktenov...99
Layj, village....................................177
Lazarev, police officer....................101
Lej, mount.......................................188
Levitsky............................19, 133, 135
Ley Ogter..127
Leyli school....................................106
Lezghins...........................129, 131, 166
Liaoyang...183
Lileyev..102
London..21
Loris Melikov M. 22
Lov, village.....................................166
Macedonia...183
Madagiz, village.............................116
Madan Bazaar....................165, 168, 169
Madrid, hotel....................................27
Magadan..112
Magazinnaya Street (now Suleyman
 Rustam Street)..............................98
Mahmud..52
Malama..................129, 130, 132, 134,
 ......146, 147, 153, 154, 157, 159, 160
Mammadgulu bey.............................39
Mankus, village...........................49, 51
Mashoryans..................................81, 82
Mauser Rifles.........................156, 176
Mavag, village..................................63
Mayilov's house.........................96, 101
Mazraa, village.................................75
Mediterranean Sea..........................145
Mehrali Zeynal oglu........................127
Mehri, village...................177, 184, 188
Melek, village.................................177
Melikshahnazarov, Aslan bey
 Melikshahnazarov.....................63, 64
Merkurevskaya Street (now Z. Aliyev
 Street)..98

INDEX

Meshedi Aghahuseyn Molla Hasan oglu.................31
Meshedi Gambar.................52
Meshedi Gulu Agamuhammad oglu....31
Meshedi Hasan.................39
Meshedi Mustafa oglu.................100
Meshedi Rzagulu Zeynal oglu.........131
Mesrop.................143, 145
Mikhailov, Ganja.................132
Mikhailov's house.................96
Mikhailovsky higher military-artillery school.................104
Mikhailovsky hospital, Baku.............99
Mikhailovsky hospital, Tiflis...........139
Milutinskaya Street (now T. Aliyarbeyov Street).................98
Minenevur, village.................185
Mir Bagirzade Mir Abbas.................185
Mir Suleyman Said Mustafa oglu......52
Mirza Aram bey.................164, 165, 172
Mirza Muhammadali oglu.................127
Mirzayans.................98, 113
Mkrtych, Khrimyan, Catholicos...21, 22
Mohsun, police.................128
Molla Hasan Efendi.................177, 178, 179, 181, 182, 183
Molla Nasreddin road.................67, 75
Mollajelilli.................18, 127, 128, 134
Mollalar, village.................185
Molokan Gardens (now Khagani Gardens).................28
Morskaya Street.................99, 102
Mshak, newspaper.................22
Muhammad, Prophet....50, 69, 108, 183
Muhammadali, Mirza oglu.................131
Mukhnatkin Savili.................98, 99
Mukhtarov Aga Murtuza.................14
Muradyan, Archimandrite.................146
Mursal Haji Gulu oglu.................66
Musak, newspaper.................146, 147
Musheksyan.................146

Najafgulu Aga.................91
Najafguluzade, Haji Molla.................131
Nakhalovka.................138
Nakhchivan.................19, 20, 33, 34, 36, 37, 38, 39, 41, 42, 45, 46, 80, 81, 104, 105, 164, 174
Nakhchivanskiy Jafargulu khan.........34
Nalbandov Sergey.................101
Namisa, village.................116
Nasiya, village.................145
Nasrullayev Jafar.................100
Nazveran, village.................55
Nehramov Aram bey.................175
Nerses.................184
Nicholas II.................14
Nikolayevskaya Street.................138
Norashen, village.................177
Noy Bayazid district.................148
Nugadi, village.................180
Nukha district.................20
Nur Muhammad's mill.................68
Nurdar, newspaper.................156
Nuru bey.................141

Oganesov Avetis.................134
Oganesov Davud, family.................29
Ohanesyan Mugdusi, shop.................27
Ojagli, mount.................63, 65
Okhaduz, village.................177
Okhchu, village...164, 165,175, 176, 177, 183, 185, 186, 187, 188, 189, 190, 191
Okhchu-Shabadak.21, 164, 172, 173, 174, 175, 176, 177, 180, 181, 185, 186, 188
Ordubad......48, 165, 166, 175, 179, 180, 181, 185, 186, 187, 191
Ordubadi Mammad Said....14, 16, 23, 32
Ordubadsky Mehdi khan.................36
Orlov, cossack.................128
Osipov's house.................96
Oskuyey.................184
Ottoman Empire....22, 23, 149, 150, 182
Ottoman Sultan.................182
Ovanesov Sarkis Minayevich.................28

Pakiza khanim.................165
Panahali khan.................113
Panbak province.................53
Panusluv, village.................175, 177, 183, 187, 188, 189, 190

INDEX

Panuslu-Girdekan..............................191
Papravend, village............109, 124, 125
Parapet (now Fountains Square)...96, 102
Paris...................................21, 107, 108
Parutchiyev.......................................98
Pasha Budag oglu..............................55
Paskevich, Governor-General, Irevan...39
Perov Amos...19
Persi, village......................................55
Persian, Persians...........................22, 93
Peter I..22
Petersburg......23, 34, 104, 105, 106, 107
Peterson.............................146, 153, 155
Pezmeri, village.........................174, 182
Pipis, village......................................141
Pivovarov....115, 116, 119, 120, 123, 125
Port-Arthur..84
Primorsky quarter.............................100
Purdavud, village.....174, 182, 183, 185
Purkhud, village.......................118, 120

Rafibeyov Ali Akber bey..........126, 132
Rafiyev Haji Muhammad Huseyn....128
Rakhdakhana, village.......................177
Ranik, village....................................121
Rasulbeyov Mammadrza's house.......98
Reno Company...................................31
Rilski, Major-General.......................138
Rome, Roman Empire........................22
Russia.......14, 57, 59, 79, 112, 155, 162
Russian autocracy...............................80
Russian Government..................80, 149
Russian, Russians.....17, 18, 20, 23, 26,
59, 93, 96, 97, 99, 100, 105, 110, 126,
......129, 156, 159, 162, 163, 184, 187
Russian-Japanese war in 1904-1905......
....59, 84
Russian-Turkish war in 1877-1878........
....21, 22, 183
Rustam Ismayil oglu........................134
Rza Jabrail oglu................................134

Saakyans Sabah................................113
Saakyans Stepan...............................184
Sadig Meshedi 134
Safar Muhammad Mustafa oglu.......131

Safaraliyev Kamil bey......................102
Safaraliyev's house......................99, 100
Safiyar bey..165
Saggarsu, village......178, 179, 180, 181
......................182, 185, 188, 189, 190
Sago...63, 64
Sahadur, village................................177
Sakharov............................166, 167, 168
Salanik, Turkey................................112
Saldashli, village...............................185
Salman Mehdi oglu..........................127
Salyan regiment..................................28
Samur..153
Sanjan bey..63
Sarajig, village....................................74
Sardov, village..................................184
Sarkis..139
Sarkisyan..152
Sasanids, Sasanid Empire...................22
Sasun.........................21, 79, 99, 182
Semyonov Artem..............................101
Senali, village...................................185
Serebrakov Andriyans......................131
Sergeyev brothers...............................98
Serseng..115
Serv, village..............................110, 112
Seyid Dadash oglu............................100
Shabadak..................164, 165, 181, 191
..................................185, 188, 189, 190
Shafi, Major, Muhammadgulu bey's
father...104
Shahmaliyev Muhammad bey..152, 156
Shahnazarov's house.........................100
Shakhavend, village.........................110
Shamakinsky......................................27
Shamsaddin, village..................143, 145
Sheikhmali, village......................67, 70
Sheikh-ul-Islam..............42, 46, 47, 130
Sheytan bazaar.................................138
Shikhavend, village..........................124
Shikhlar, village.................................91
Shikhli, village...................................67
Shinkov Artem...................................26
Shirazi Hafiz......................................93

199

INDEX

Shirnikin..........146
Shoragel province..........53
Shua, newspaper..........103
Shuragel..........174
Shusha.....20, 21, 60, 62, 66, 67, 68, 75, .76, 77, 78, 84, 85, 86, 88, 89, 90, 91, ...94, 109, 110, 111, 115, 121, 133, ...164, 173, 174, 175, 184
Shusha Muslims..........79, 80
Shykhmahmud, village..........33
Simonov Minas, shops..........27
Sirkhavend, village..........110, 113, 114
Sisiyan district..........33
Sistula, village..........110, 123
Smorodsky..........119
Social-Democratic Party..........138, 140
Sofulu, village..........141, 142
Sograt..........19, 63
Soldat bazaar..........138
South (Iranian) Azerbaijan..........18
Stanislavskaya Street (now Azadlyg Avenue)..........99, 102
State Duma..........22, 23
Stepanov, doctor..........146
Suleyman..........172
Suleyman, village..........74
Sultanov beys..........186
Sunni muslims..........162, 163, 182
Surakhanskaya Street (now part of Chingiz Mustafayev Street and part of Dilara Aliyeva Street)..28, 30, 97, 100
Surli, village..........74
Surmeli..........55
Sust, village..........62
Switzerland..........112, 148, 153
Tabriz..........184
Tagashvili, General..........89, 114, 128
Taghiyev Haji Zeynalabdin..........16, 18
Taghiyev's house..........27
Tagi Agahuseyn oglu..........130
Tagiyanusov..........146, 156
Tahir..........166
Talibkhanov Tapdig..........61
Tashtin, village..........177

Tatar Hasan..........75
Tatli, village..........142, 144, 145
Tekhmichenko..........98
Tekya, village..........55, 56
Telefonnaya Street (now 28 May Street)..........100, 101, 102
Terasayev Alexander's house..........100
Ter-Avanesov..........146
Teroganesov Israil..........66
Ter-Petrosyan's house..........101
Ter-Sarkisov's shop..........138
Terter..........114, 115, 120, 123
Terter Gorge..........109, 120
Ter-Yapramov..........128
Teshtikh, mountain..........190
Teyvant..........153
Teze Heyat ("New Life"), newspaper...16
Tezekend..........51, 52
The Khalatovs..........37
Tiflis......18, 42, 90, 104, 107, 108, 126, ...136, 137, 138, 140, 146, 161
Tiflis peaceful talks..........22
Tiflisskiy listok ("Tiflis leaflet"), newspaper..........158
Tirjabat, village..........49, 51
Tirol..........148
Tiyunov Grigor..........127
Tokhana, village..........127, 135
Tokyo..........112
Topchubashov Alimardan bey..146, ...153, 157
Torgovaya Street (now Nizami Street)..........99
Traubenberg, Rausch von..........138
Tsarist Russia..........59
Tsitsianovskaya Street (now Tebriz Khelilbeyli Street)..........26, 29
Tumanov Sevan..........144
Tunbul, village..........34
Turkey..........21, 22, 23, 27, 57, 79, ...112, 182, 183, 184
Turkmenchay treaty..........22
Tutya, village..........52
Uchkilse (Three Churches)..........53, 60

INDEX

Ujanabus, village..............................177
Ulkhu...165
Umudlu, village............110, 120, 121,
.................................122, 123, 125
Unus, village....................................174
USA..21
Usereng, village................................177
Ushu, village................................53, 54
Vabayjan..63
Vachisyans..184
Van..21, 182
Varshapetov's house............................98
Vartanyans Karapet..........................184
Varvara..184
Veisalli, village................58, 62, 63, 76
Vekilov Ibrahim aga.........................152
Vekilov Muhammad aga..................146
Velistan...183
Veliyev Aghadadash...........................28
Vendean events, France....................162
Veng, village................................81, 177
Verdiyev, Abbas Huseyn oglu...........131
Vevren, Lt Col....................................90
Vezirov Hashim bey............................16
Vezirov Isfendiyar bey 66, 67
Vorontsov-Dashkov I.I., Count, Viceroy
of the Caucasus..................18, 19, 42,
..............101, 106, 138, 146, 159, 161
Vorontsov Square..............................138
Vorontsova, Duchess...........................90
Vorontsovskaya, street (now General
Azizbeyov Street............................26

Vuri, village......................................145
Yaglivend, village........................58, 64
Yaradullu, village......................142, 144
Yarimja, village.........................110, 123
Yazid...71
Yegayev Yerivant's garden...............128
Yegintin, Police officer..........96, 98, 99
Yegizarov's house...............................96
Yemezli, village................................185
Yevlakh...91
Yukhary Gezlek, village.....................76
Yuri Antonovich...............................100
Yusifbeyov Bakhish bey...........110, 118
Yusifzade Mirza Jamal.......................57
Zafski, village...................................145
Zagatala..153
Zakharbeyov Mirza..........................113
Zangilan..168
Zarisli, village..............................82, 91
Zengezur.........19, 21, 90 110, 119, 148,
..............164, 173, 174, 185, 187, 190
Zengezur regiment..............................63
Zeyam...142
Zeynalov's house..............................100
Zeytun........................21, 79, 182, 184
Zhbilyay, Governor General, Tiflis..136
Ziyadkhanov Adil khan...........146, 153,
....157, 160
Zurnabad, village..............................135
Zurum, village..................................185

MAMMAD SAID ORDUBADI

YEARS OF BLOOD

A History of the Armenian-Muslim Clashes
in the Caucasus, 1905-1906